SOCIAL SECURITY
HORROR STORIES

PROTECT YOURSELF FROM THE SYSTEM & AVOID CLAWBACKS

by
Laurence Kotlikoff
Professor of Economics, Boston University

and

Terry Savage
Financial Columnist and Author,
The Savage Truth on Money

To the millions of Americans who have contributed faithfully to Social Security all their working lives, and who deserve better treatment.

Contents

Introduction.. v

PART 1
Social Security Nightmares 1

  1 Nightmares by the Numbers 3

  2 The Claw in Your Mailbox............................. 11

  3 Welcome to Clawback Hell............................ 21

  4 Terrorizing Teachers and Other Public Servants............. 29

  5 Impoverishing the Disabled.......................... 39

  6 The Claw from the Grave 55

  7 A Final Clawback Horror Story....................... 67

PART 2
Social Security Scams 71

  8 Social Security's Foundational Scam 73

  9 The Use-It-or-Lose-It Scam.......................... 83

  10 The Widows Scam 91

  11 The Retirement Trap Scam.......................... 101

  12 The Contribute-for-Nothing Scam.................... 111

  13 The Benefit Taxation Scam.......................... 115

  14 The Take-Your-Benefits-Early Scam 121

  15 The Crazy Calculator Scam......................... 125

  16 The Employer Contribution Scam.................... 131

  17 Social Security's Sexism Scam...................... 135

PART 3
**Avoiding Your Personal and Our
Collective Social Security Horror Stories** 147

  18 Don't Trust Social Security 149

  19 The Appeals Process—or *non*-Process.............. 157

  20 Keep Your Own Records 161

  21 Social Security Is Dysfunctional..................... 167

Conclusion: Action is the Only Reaction 175

CLAWBACK LETTER

You received $38,129.00 more in Social Security benefits than you were due.

You were not due benefits for June 2014 through November 2014, January 2015 through February 2015, and April 2015 through February 2017. You wer not due benefits due to your substantial earnings.

How To Pay Us Back

Please refund this overpayment within 30 days. Make your check or money order payable to "Social Security Administration". Include the Social Security Claim Number on the check or money order, and send it to us in the enclosed envelope.

If you pay us by check or money order, make sure the check or money order is in United States (U.S.) dollars or in local currency equal to U.S. dollars. When you pay us in local currency, we use the exchange rates in effect at the time we get your payment. If this causes a difference between the amount you pay us and the amount you owe us, we will let you know. If you cannot mail your payment to us, please contact your nearest Federal Benefits Unit (FBU). Visit www.ssa.gov/foreign/foreign.htm for a list of FBUs. If you ar in Canada, visit www.ssa.gov/foreign/canada.htm to find the office that services your area. They will help you make the refund.

If we do not receive your refund within 30 days, we plan to recover the overpayment by withholding your full benefit starting with the payment you would normally receive about August 24, 2022. We will continue withholding your benefit until we fully recover the overpayment.

SEE NEXT PAGE

Introduction

Social Security was created out of a dream to make all Americans' lives far more secure. The initial goal was that no older American would live in poverty. That dream has turned into an actual or potential nightmare for each of us—old or young, rich or poor, healthy or disabled. The nightmare comes in a letter clawing back benefits that Social Security says it paid out in error.

Social Security is quietly issuing hundreds of thousands of clawback letters every year. Its 2022 Annual Trustees Report says recipients collectively owe $21.6 billion because of Social Security's mistaken overpayments.

Compared to Social Security's total yearly outlays, $21.6 billion is a small number. But it is a financial disaster for those who depend on their monthly benefit. Even worse, Social Security's demand letter comes with no explanation, no proof, no accounting for their error. Instead, it comes with a demand for immediate repayment—or the threat that the money will be withheld from future benefit checks, tax refunds, wages, or whatever they can grab in a lawsuit.

At any point in time, millions of households are experiencing or contesting Social Security's basic rule: *Our mistake is your problem.* In other words, when Social Security makes a mistake, it bears no responsibility or cost. You are the one who must repay—immediately out of your savings or through cuts in your future Social Security benefit checks. In fact, you may never have personally filed for Social Security and still receive a clawback letter!

Since Social Security bears no cost for its egregious mistakes, it has absolutely no incentive to fix its software and train its staff to get things right. Its mistakes cost the system vital resources and billions in administrative dollars—funds needed to help cover Social Security's huge financial shortfall.

The clawback letters can be for $175 dollars or $304,122—actual clawback amounts we have seen. They can arrive soon after benefits begin, or 45 years later. They can come for benefits you technically received at age 2, for which your now-deceased parents applied. The clawback letter can appear the month your husband dies, announcing that your widow's benefit isn't coming for the next 18 years in order to recover excessive retirement benefits paid to the spouse you buried last week.

These demands fall particularly hard on the poorest among us—senior citizens who depend on their monthly checks for basic needs and disabled families who have no other source of income. Confiscating benefits when recipients are unable to work can represent a financial death sentence. Minorities are disproportionately poor and, thus, disproportionately victimized.

Clawback letters all have common denominators—deadlines, threats to cut current or future benefits, and no justification. Each letter is admitting a mistake. But with no explanation, no one can tell whether the alleged mistake is, itself, a mistake.

Everyone grabbed by Social Security's merciless claw is in the same boat—powerless to deal with a bureaucracy that violates all norms of due process and provides no explanation of its actions. It's a bureaucracy that rarely responds—leaves you on hold for hours, schedules calls that never come, always deflects responsibility, and keeps no records of your case.

This book confronts the system that is quietly overwhelming our most vulnerable citizens and, indeed, all of us. It's also about terrible scams Social Security is running, of which few are aware. These include the widows scam, the use-it-or-lose-it scam, the earnings test scam, and the take-your-benefits-early scam, not to mention Social Security's incredibly sexist provisions. Some can cost you a small fortune over your lifetime. All are intrinsically linked to Social Security's foundational financing scam and all are described here, along with advice on protecting yourself.

This book is not about addressing the future solvency of the Social Security system, which its trustees have clearly revealed. Yes, within a decade—unless substantial reforms are made by Congress—Social Security will find itself unable to pay out promised benefits in full. That comes as no surprise. Instead, we want to reveal *today's* horror stories—happening to your mother, father, child or friend—even as we write this book. Left unchecked, you may be the next victim. These are outrages that can and must be confronted immediately.

We are two distinct voices who find ourselves in perfect harmony when it comes to sounding these alarms. We both seek to fix Social Security, not end it. We both think a well-functioning Social Security system is essential. But so much of what's going on under Social Security's hood makes a mockery of the system's title, specifically the word "security."

We both write for the public about personal finance. Larry Kotlikoff is a Boston University economist, and Terry Savage is a nationally syndicated columnist. We learned about clawbacks from readers describing their personal horror stories. Over time, we realized that the stories coming our way were just the tip of the iceberg—that millions of Americans were being clawed back and caught in Social Security's impenetrable bureaucracy. As for scams, we are both students of the system. We know all the good the system is doing and precisely where its bodies are buried. It's time to pinpoint those graves.

To reiterate, this book is not about all the well-publicized concerns over the future solvency of Social Security. Instead, it is about the dysfunction of the current system that is causing massive financial pain for so many Americans. We do, however, expose the system's original sin—lying about the nature of its financing. One lie begets another, and the system's original lie turned deception into a basic operating principle.

Avoiding Your Personal Horror Story in Three Parts

Our book has three parts. The first, written by Terry, details personal horror stories that are truly unbelievable. We're not writing a Steven King novel. This is nonfiction. We're letting you know precisely what's happening—*in the actual words of clawback victims*—to so many of us every day.

Part Two, written by Larry, is about Social Security's aforementioned terrible scams that are secretly harming millions of us and our children—being induced to check an extra box on a form and losing hundreds of thousands of dollars in future benefits; making a lifetime of Social Security "contributions" in exchange for not a single red penny of extra benefits; remarrying a day before age 60 and losing widow(er)s benefits from your deceased former spouse; being conned into not returning to work under threat of a massive tax that's isn't. And the list goes on.

Part Three is our combined advice on how to avoid clawbacks and the system's other traps. Indeed, there are simple steps you can take to avoid your own horror story. This will require a bit of work on your part. You'll need to create your own assessment of benefits owed instead of relying on Social Security.

Your efforts will provide a huge payoff. You will know that the benefits you receive are exactly what you are owed. The computations will be easy once you input your information into the inexpensive user-friendly tool, MaximizeMySocialSecurity.com, which was developed by Larry. It can tell if you are being overpaid or underpaid if you're already collecting, as well as what you should receive once you start collecting.

Other commercial programs may also get these calculations right, at least in simple cases. But you need to act before the error adds up to a small fortune—your retirement fortune. Social Security may take 45 years to figure out a mistake. The amount of a clawback can be astronomical—$304K is the highest we've seen to date.

We prescribe remedies for this unacceptable failure of process in the Social Security agency. Some involve money to update the creaking computer systems that fail to gather information and track its processes. But other fixes involve the leadership of this important agency, to create a culture of service and training that enables hard-working employees to fulfill the agency's pledge to provide superior customer service. In that regard, we recommend Social Security create an ombudsman's office, similar to the Taxpayer Assistance Center at the

IRS, where problems can be resolved immediately, understanding that time is of the essence.

We're also going to enlist you in a collective mission—ending Social Security's financial malfeasance, including the system's Ponzi scheme that's threatening to ruin our retirements and bankrupt our children. Through our joint efforts, Social Security can be the system we revere, not the system we fear.

Let us tell you more about our background so you'll know we are here to protect you.

Larry and Terry

Larry is a Boston University professor of economics. As his Kotlikoff. net website makes clear, Larry works on everything from climate change to healthcare to tax reform. But his passion, exemplified by his software company and latest and award-winning book, *Money Magic— an Economist's Guide to More Money, Less Risk, and a Better Life*, is conveying economics-based personal finance. He's on a mission to help people plan their finances properly, as economics and common sense prescribe. In 2022, he was honored with the SABEW award for *Money Magic*, the top personal finance book of the year.

Larry founded his software company, Economic Security Planning, Inc., in 1993. He's never taken a penny of salary. He works for free for two reasons—to better compensate his employees (full disclosure: including two relatives) and to keep the prices of his company's software tools as low as possible. His best-selling book, *Get What's Yours: the Secrets to Maxing Out Your Social Security*, was co-authored by Larry, Paul Solman of *PBS NewsHour*, and Phil Moeller, longtime personal finance journalist.

Terry is the best-selling author of *The Savage Truth on Money* and a nationally syndicated personal finance columnist for Chicago Tribune content agency. She has won a National Press Club award for her financial reporting. Terry appears regularly on WGN-TV and WGN-Radio in Chicago, and is a frequent guest on national news programs. She is a registered investment advisor, and was a founding member and the first woman trader on the Chicago Board Options Exchange, as well as a trader on the Chicago Mercantile Exchange, where she now serves on the Board of Directors of CME Group. Her weekly columns are designed to demystify the financial markets and planning decisions. Terry answers money questions on the "Ask Terry" section of her website, TerrySavage.com.

We have each dedicated our lives to helping people make smart money decisions. This book is an extension of our mission.

Grab a Drink

Our first story comes from a victim who emailed Terry. She could be you, your mother, or your grandmother—now or in a few years. This is one of many, many emails we received that made us realize we needed to understand the magnitude of the system's clawbacks and other problems. So we both started writing columns—Larry on his Substack newsletter, larrykotlikoff.substack.com, and Terry in her syndicated column and posted at TerrySavage.com—asking readers to send us their horror stories.

Here's that first email from a widow named Ruth who was horrified at a notice from Social Security telling her they had made a mistake and were clawing back $88,000 of benefits, potentially forcing her to sell her home.

In May 2021 I received a letter from Social Security stating I owe $88,734 dollars because I was not entitled to my husband's benefits because I collect a pension. I went through all the process with the SS office, brought in all documents that were needed by them and nothing was ever told to me by them that I was not able to collect. I filed an appeal but never heard from them until now!

I am 73 and had a heart attack with triple bypass done. I don't want to lose my house!! I have all documents since this began almost 2 years ago. With COVID they never would get back to me and offices were always closed. Now they are threatening me. Please help!

Ruth is not alone. Millions of seniors and disabled people are facing this nightmare. We will tell you their stories—and more. In fact, we continue to collect these stories at our website, www.SocialSecurity HorrorStories.com, where you can post your personal experience and get updated on our latest efforts to pressure the Agency and Congress to make changes.

PART 1

Social Security Nightmares

CHAPTER 1

Nightmares by the Numbers

Social Security pays out more than $1 trillion in benefits every year to some 70 million recipients. Most of the money goes to retirees and disabled workers. The rest is paid to their spouses, children, survivors, and former spouses. There are even benefits for dependent parents of deceased workers. About 11 percent of the payouts from Social Security go to disabled workers as well as their spouses and dependents. An additional 7.7 million people receive Supplemental Security Income (SSI), which provides income support to needy persons aged 65 or older, blind or disabled adults, and blind or disabled children.

You'd expect a system this big to make some mistakes. But Social Security makes routine mistakes—hundreds of thousands of mistakes every year—mistakes that financially terrorize millions of Americans, many of whom are already living desperate economic lives. Unfortunately, those terrorized millions may include you—either today or tomorrow.

The numbers are mind-boggling. We call them MEGO-numbers. That stands for "My Eyes Glaze Over." But when it comes down to *your* monthly benefit check, the numbers become very personal. Social Security estimates that 37 percent of men and 42 percent of women receive 50 percent or more of their income from Social Security. Approximately 15 percent of recipients rely on their monthly benefit check for 90 percent of their income. A clawback or a cutback can mean the difference between food and medicine, between rent or homelessness.

What's the Root Cause of These Mistakes?

It starts with Social Security's mind-boggling complexity. The system provides only 12 benefits. Yet its handbook has 2,728 rules about those 12 benefits. And its Program Operations Manual System has literally hundreds of thousands of rules about the 2,728 rules about the 12 benefits.

Google "SSA POMS" and start clicking on its links within links within links, which seem to go on endlessly. There are so many that Social Security doesn't bother numbering them. Hence, no one actually knows the precise number of stipulations, caveats, exceptions, provisions, Catch 22s—call them what you will—governing the 2,728 rules about the 12 benefits.

Perhaps someday a political scientist will do a careful study. But our hunch is that Social Security constitutes the most convoluted, byzantine set of provisions, regulations, and restrictions that mankind has yet devised under the heading "public policy." This is the "magnificent" achievement of members of Congress, congressional lawyers, and Social Security bureaucrats, who have worked tirelessly for decades to construct a fiscal program that no one—including no one at Social Security—can fully understand.

Such complexity is not ordained by the gods when it comes to designing a country's old-age security policy. New Zealand's retirement benefit (superannuation) system has just one rule. Reach age 65 and receive a monthly check—the same check everyone else over 65 receives. How long does your check last? It ends when you end—full stop.

The Number and Magnitude
of Social Security Mistakes

In 2021, Social Security sent 223,500 Americans clawback letters notifying them that they had been overpaid—most, it seems, for years, some for decades. The terrifying letters run like this: "We overpaid you $X. Pay back the $X immediately or have your benefits stopped in full or in part." In just that one year, they added $8.6 billion in newly discovered clawbacks, bringing their outstanding repayment demands to a total of $21.6 billion. By the time you read this, the receivables will be substantially higher.

Social Security points out that its payment accuracy rates are high. Indeed, the percentage of mistakes might seem small when you consider that Social Security paid out more than $1.1 trillion in benefits that year. But to the recipients, who had already spent those retirement or disability payments, the amounts are certainly not trivial.

Your individual clawback amount could be $4,000, $35,000, or $300,000. Regardless of size, all clawbacks share a common denominator. The pay-or-else letter comes with no precise or even cursory explanation of the source of the overpayment. And, by definition, this clawback comes at a time when most Social Security beneficiaries are too old, or too disabled, to go back to work and earn the money to pay off this demand.

Here's what goes through your mind when you open one of these heartless and terrible letters:

Is Social Security accusing me of fraud? Am I about to be hauled into court? Or did that young staffer I spoke to on the phone 10 years ago get something wrong? I told them to include that critical information. Could they have failed to enter it into the computer? Did they discover a mistake in my work record or suddenly credit my contributions to someone else? Maybe they didn't update my record when I married and changed names? Did the local school system, where I taught for eleven years, not transmit my pension amount to Social Security? The school system didn't participate in Social Security, meaning my Social Security benefit is supposed to be docked based on my pension.

All this goes through your brain in rapid succession as your blood pressure heads toward stroke territory. Then you erupt. "What the hell is going on? Let me call Social Security!"

Next, you pick up the phone and spend hours on hold only to be connected with someone who's been on the job for seven months and

Social Security Administration Annual Report, Fiscal Year 2022

According to SSA, in FY 2022, it recovered over $4.7 billion in overpayments at an administrative cost of $0.06 on average for every dollar collected. Still, at the end of the FY, SSA had a $21.6-billion uncollected overpayment balance (see Figure 5).

Figure 5: FY 2021 Overpayment Recovery

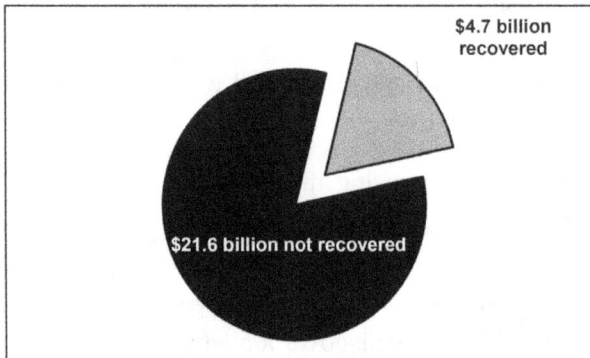

$4.7 billion recovered

$21.6 billion not recovered

PROGRESS THE SOCIAL SECURITY ADMINISTRATION HAS MADE

In FY 2019, SSA established the Improper Payment Prevention Team to address improper payments; it has developed strategies to determine the underlying causes of payment errors, develop corrective action plans, and determine cost-effective actions. In FY 2022, SSA continued monitoring the progress of mitigation strategies and corrective actions.

has no clue. But this customer support representative sets up a phone appointment in a month with a person who does know. When that day and hour arrive—which you've been focused on every minute of every day because your entire financial future is at stake—lo and behold, they don't call.

Welcome to Social Security hell. This is only the first circle of hell. In the coming weeks, months, and even years, you will be introduced not only to the non-callback circle, but also to the lost documents circle, the not-in-this-office circle, the our-computers-are down circle, and the you-mistakenly—checked-this-box-so-too-bad-for-you circles of hell. You are caught in the downward spiral that destroys your peace of mind and your financial well-being.

Once you have become a target, the "you" in the "we overpaid you" message is not necessarily you. It could reference benefits paid to your mom on your behalf when you were a toddler and she was disabled. Now you're age 25. Your mom is dead. Social Security decides, after all this time, that it made a mistake.

The logic behind their clawback claim: Since those benefits were intended for your use, you—at age two—should have known it was an overpayment and set Social Security straight. In any case, it's time to pay up. If you don't, they will take action. That could include garnishing your current wages or reducing your future Social Security benefits.

Can You Appeal?

Want to appeal? Of course, you can. But be aware that more than half of appeals are quickly denied. Here's the attitude you're up against:

> Be our guest. In a few weeks, we'll almost surely reject your request for reconsideration. Then you have 60 days to appeal your case to one of our hand-picked, fully in our pockets "judges." They'll get to your case. It may take a year if you're lucky, two years if you're not, but eventually they'll get to you. Meanwhile, if you're currently receiving a check—be it your retirement benefit, a widow's benefit, a disabled child benefit, or any of our 12 benefits—we'll immediately, starting next month, cut or stop your payment.

If you are among the most vulnerable and surviving on Social Security, this clawback can literally condemn you to extreme poverty and an early death. The administrative law judge chosen and paid by the agency can later decide—long after you've been cut off or cut down—that either Social Security screwed up, or that cutting your benefit will defeat the purpose of the Social Security Act, and belatedly grant you a waiver. But by then, you've lived years in penury.

Or your appeal may be approved if you weren't at fault and if "equity and good conscience" requires dropping the clawback. Sadly, the record of successful appeals is dismal. In Part 3, we'll discuss these two ways to contest your treatment as well as how to try to get in front of a federal judge to adjudicate your case—a judge not on Social Security's payroll.

Social Security's Mistakes Put Us All at Risk

Don't think that Social Security's gnarled clawback letter won't show up in your mailbox. That letter is not: "Hey, we probably goofed up and overpaid you. Please call this number and we'll sort things out. Unfortunately, you may owe us some money." On the contrary, it's: "You owe us $37,527. Pay up— or else we will grab it any way we can."

And despite the agency's proclamation that no clawbacks will be made until an appeal is resolved, Social Security is routinely cutting, if not eliminating, current recipients' benefits to reclaim money that it claims, but doesn't care to prove, it overpaid.

Not Only Immoral, but Likely Illegal

By the time Social Security discovers its own mistake, the overpayments it claims it made have likely been spent on basic necessities. Paying back spent money is generally extremely difficult if not impossible for most clawback victims. And withholding future benefits because of the agency's own mistakes, years after the alleged mistakes were made, is, quite frankly, immoral.

When asked about this practice, Social Security responds: "The Social Security Act requires us to adjust or recover benefits when an overpayment occurs. An overpayment is the difference between the amount paid to the overpaid individual and the amount to which the individual was entitled."

Is there no room for common sense or compassion in the application of the Social Security Act?

In fact, there *is* room for Social Security to avoid these capricious confiscations. In three different sections of their regulations, specifically in § 416.554 of its Code of Federal Regulations, there is reference to the term "against equity and good conscience." That waiver is to be applied in situations "where the individual changed his or her position for the worse, or relinquished a valuable right because of reliance upon a notice that payment would be made or because of the incorrect payment itself."

For example, this reliance would apply when a Social Security recipient decided to retire based on the benefits Social Security told the recipient he or she would receive. And it would equally apply to other work and life decisions made based on benefits a recipient was told to expect, or was actually receiving, from Social Security. Everything from taking another job to spending money on a new car or vacation would be impacted by a person's reliance on income provided by or expected from Social Security benefits. And certainly, that person never expected to receive a huge bill for repayment of benefits at this stage of his or her life.

In 1992, the Ninth Circuit Court of Appeals ruled that this term of "against equity and good conscience" should be broadly applied, based on the case of a person "who was without fault in receiving these payments."

If an attorney were to bring a class-action suit for the millions of Americans who have been clawed back already to the tune of billions just this past year, and all those currently in process of being clawed back, the court ruling in the case of *Quinlivan v. Sullivan* would provide the perfect legal justification.

Clawing back benefits from dependent retirees and disabled persons because of mistakes made solely by the Social Security Administration is clearly "against equity and good conscience."

CHAPTER 2

The Claw in Your Mailbox

et's start with a simple premise: Few people come to Social Security knowing what their benefits *should* be. (The exceptions are those who use Larry's MaximizeMySocialSecurity.com software, described later in this book, or equally accurate commercial software.) Instead, most people come to Social Security to ask about the amount of their benefits. And they likely ask for advice about their claiming choices.

Now let's add one more basic premise to our discussion: Most of the people who come to Social Security asking for help are either seniors about to claim retirement benefits or disabled people who may have other challenges and health issues. In other words, they are likely the least sophisticated about technology and the most likely to need help.

And a final premise: People don't come to Social Security to claim benefits unless they believe that they are entitled to something based on their work record, or that of a spouse, an ex-spouse, or a parent. They correctly assume they are entitled to a benefit because they or their current or former relative contributed to the program over the years.

Bottom line: Those who contact Social Security are almost always dependent on the information and advice given to them by the telephone representatives and online calculators at www.ssa.gov.

Customer Service?

Given this, you would think that Social Security would have learned a bit about customer service over the 88 years of its existence. It certainly gives lip service to the concept. Its home page at ssa.gov proclaims:

> "We are passionate about supporting our customers by delivering financial support, providing superior customer service, and ensuring the safety and security of your information."

The reality falls far short of this lofty mission. When you call your car dealership for service, the company immediately brings up your service record—tracking your last oil change or brake repair. You would think Social Security could just as easily set up tracking files of all their decisions about a claimant's benefits. Social Security says it records all telephone conversations, yet even when requested, it cannot find them to adjudicate blame for wrong advice.

You would think each employee would have a badge number or direct phone extension contact number to make follow-up easier. You would think Social Security would hire people who know that their job is to serve their clients—the claimants—and give employees the tools to make their work easier.

But despite its stated mission, Social Security appears to have no training program that prioritizes this supposed commitment to serve its dependent clientele. In fact, far too many Americans will tell you that their experiences with Social Security are beyond awful. And they have sent us their horror stories to prove it.

Throughout this book their stories are told in their own words, with their own spelling and punctuation, only lightly edited for length. Their emotion shows through, and it is mostly pain.

Jean's Story

My name is Jean, I applied online for Social Security in June, 2014 and was told I'd receive $1,903/mo. Thinking this was high, I asked for a recalculation from our local office and was told it was correct.

In June 2018 they told me it was too high and should have been $422/mo. They wanted the overpayment of $72,343 in 30 days. I appealed but could never get to an administrative hearing. They told me I would get one in October 2019 and restarted my monthly payments, only to stop them again in 2021 because no hearing was held.

Then in July 2022 they indicated they would send additional information regarding a hearing, but it never came. They are still garnishing my benefit, which now includes my spousal benefit on my husband's monthly benefit. To date I have repaid approx. $21,800.

The frustrating part of this is that they twice told me the original $1,903 was correct, and I accepted the benefit based on their confirmation. Now I won't receive a benefit until I'm 76. Thank you for anything you can do!

If Social Security doesn't get the correct calculation at the start, you will be drawn into the vortex of darkness and financial destruction. Social Security made the original mistake. And many subsequent mistakes. And with its power over your current and future benefits, you will continue to suffer while it endlessly shuffles the problem around internally.

Social Security's Complexity and Information Requirements Breed Mistakes

Of the many sources of Social Security mistakes, human error by Social Security's staff may be the most important. Social Security's underpaid, undertrained, overwhelmed, and, far too often, uncaring staff are totally overmatched by this bureaucratic morass. In Larry's experience (based on years of interacting with beneficiaries who contacted Social Security), most staffers' answers to even simple questions are either wrong, incomplete, or misleading. Since many, if not most, benefit applications are done over the phone, staffer filing mistakes are routine.

Worse, applicants can't immediately double-check what's been done on their behalf. And since applicants presume their cases have been handled properly, they almost never closely examine the cryptic letters from Social Security that may provide clues to mistakes that were committed.

Another major source of Social Security mistakes is failure of Social Security's computer to communicate with the IRS's computer on a timely basis—*or* even attempt to collect critical data from pension providers. Take someone who is receiving a pension from noncovered employment—a job at which Social Security FICA taxes are not deducted. The size of this benefit can, via application of the Windfall Elimination Provision (WEP) and Government Pension Offset (GPO), discussed in Chapter 4, affect both Social Security retirement and excess dependent, widow, and divorcee benefits. But if the IRS doesn't transmit 1099s to Social Security specifying these non-covered pensions, which it doesn't, the beneficiary won't be WEP'd or GPO'd until Social Security receives the information, often by accident and often years, if not decades later.

Another channel for benefit overpayments involves Social Security's earnings test. Workers subject to this provision must report their earnings on a timely basis for Social Security to properly dock their benefits on a timely basis. Of course, doing so is no guarantee that the Social Security staffer will enter your information on a timely basis.

Then there's the problem of earning a few dollars too much to continue to qualify for your disability insurance benefit or Supplemental Security Income. Beneficiaries who are receiving either of these benefits may be suffering from mental health problems. For these people, keeping track of precisely what they are earning in a given month and what they need to tell Social Security may be physically impossible. Yet, Social Security has no leeway for mistakes. Social Security is Uncle Scrooge personified to the hilt—as cold and calculating as a computer can get.

Speaking of computers, who knows if Social Security's software is getting complex calculations right. As discussed below, Social Security's computers have been known to produce strange results. On one occasion, the system's computer mailed out millions of patently incorrect benefit statements.

Indeed, in some situations with very complex benefit calculations the computations are literally done by hand! As an example, their computers don't seem programed to deal with complexity that involves several dependents trying to collect on a worker's record (e.g., a widow and three children, where the widow is subject to the earnings test and GPO and the family benefit maximum comes into play). In those cases, staffers at three different offices can readily come up with three different benefit amounts. If, years later, someone or the system's software double-checks these manual calculations and finds they were made incorrectly, we have another clawback letter heading someone's way.

Mis-Tracking Your Contributions

Social Security may not have the computing power to make correct benefit decisions, but it should be easy to track your earnings and contributions over the years, right? Wrong again.

First, let's get one thing clear: Yes, it's a contribution. That's what FICA stands for: **F**ederal **I**nsurance **C**ontributions **A**ct. You—and your employer—have been contributing a significant amount to Social Security every year.

Currently, you "contribute" 6.2 percent of all income up to $160,200. Employers deduct the tax from paychecks and "match it" (effectively taking another 6.2 percent out of what you earn), so that 12.4 percent goes to the program for each employee. If you're self-employed, you'll transmit the total 12.4 percent yourself. That's in addition to a 2.9 percent Medicare tax.

Those numbers have changed over the years, of course. The current tax rate of 6.2 percent has been in effect since 1990. But the taxable wage base was only $51,300 in 1990. In 2023, the taxable wage base is $160,200.

The common wisdom is that Social Security has kept careful track of your contributions to Social Security every year and that you can find a correct record of those contributions when you create a My Social Security account at www.ssa.gov.

But we have heard from people whose contributions have been commingled with others, who found out that an undocumented immigrant had used their SS number, or who shared the same SS number with another person for years, an error caused in the initial SS number designation.

The most fundamental issue here is that the most basic computer systems don't work well enough for Social Security to have a fair chance at getting it right. Should we blame Congress for not appropriating more money? Actually, Social Security is supposed to be self-funding. And as part of its responsibility, it should have been updating systems long ago. But, because Social Security is rarely questioned about its systems and isn't punished for its errors, the agency hasn't been forced to make changes.

Surely, a government organization tracking the lifetime earnings records of every working American should be able to deal with these basic responsibilities. Wrong again. Read on for stories of what happens when Social Security gets its most basic responsibility wrong— for a lifetime—despite desperate attempts to get this problem resolved.

Social Security Mistakes
Impact Medicare Coverage

Lest you think that Social Security's disorganized mess stops with your monthly check, consider this horror story from Carol:

> *The short story is that Social Security applied my payments ($4788.70) for my Medicare Part B premiums to my husband's Medicare account (he was not and is still not on Medicare) from April 2016 through October 2017 and they have never refunded me the money. That means this started six years ago.*
>
> *My husband is younger than I am and was not on Medicare. He received health insurance from his employer and still does.*

In May 2016 Social Security switched my Medicare benefits from my Social Security number to my husband's Social Security number. Neither Medicare nor Social Security ever told me they did this. My husband was not on Medicare and still received health insurance from his employer.

I did not realize they were doing this until I received a new Medicare card in January 2019 that showed I had only Part A coverage and that I no longer had Part B. I never received a letter from Medicare or Social Security telling me my Part B coverage had been canceled.

Once I learned my Part B had been canceled, I had to purchase private insurance ($1652) to make sure I still had health insurance. I also continued to pay my Medigap insurance ($2135) and Part D private premiums ($193) for the five months I was without coverage.

Since then, I have paid every premium on time either with a personal check or with automatic withdrawal from my checking account and later directly through my Social Security benefits. Many premiums have been paid twice just to make sure my Medicare was not canceled again.

I have received multiple letters from Social Security advising me of additional money I owe on my Medicare account. When I have called to inquire about these letters, I have always received answers that made no sense. No one would ever give me an explanation. There is no way I can figure out how they have calculated their numbers. I have repeatedly asked for documents to explain their calculations and have been told the documents were for their use and I could not have any of them . . . I have a 2" thick stack of documents about this problem. The problem has not been resolved. This is never ending.

Social Security Answers to No One

Clearly, an initial problem with Social Security benefits can spiral out of your control. Wrap your brain and heart around what this woman has been going through for years:

I'm disabled since around 2005. I never wanted to stay on disability. I was in my young 20s when I became disabled, and I had made decent money considering my age. I made every effort to return to work. I went back to college, which was extremely difficult for me. Upon recommendation from SSA, I followed regulation 404.1028 which states that if you are going to school at a university and work at the university at the same time it's not considered employment so long as the work doesn't pertain to your career goal/path. So, I did just that. They came back and claimed it was employment.

They stopped my checks and claimed I owed around $3400. I didn't agree but they blackmailed me by stopping my checks completely. I made a payment plan and stuck with it.

Then they came back with a change and gave me a check for over $14,000. That lady retired and new staff clawed it back and demanded more money. Every time I reached out to them to resolve, the bill suddenly went higher.

No additional work was ever done. I reached out to congressman several times only to have my bill grow by around $1000 each time. I was told by SSA staff in Cleburne, Texas that local office policy is to NEVER give money back AND that local office policy trumps regulations, so they don't have to follow them.

To this day NO ONE will discuss regulation 404.1028 with me. They refused dozens of attempts to request an in-person meeting to discuss or work through the problems. Yet, on the phone, they won't discuss the regulations either. They say they don't have access.

They tell me they are too busy to discuss the issues with me. I had an appeal pending for over four years. Way before the pandemic.

I have documentation from SSA showing so much confusion: multiple times where I'd receive 3 different letters in the same week with different amounts and dates less than 7 days apart, a lump sum check given to them for over $14,000 and the month of the payment keeps changing in their system (computers don't do that), over $40,000 in money paid back according to SSA 1099s and they still want $7500 more. They owe me over $40,000!

Collective Action is the Answer

If you're feeling sick to your stomach, hold on. It gets worse. The nightmares that our supposedly benign and beloved institution is inflicting on millions of us are truly beyond belief. Worse, the financial and psychological abuse has no end in sight.

Actually, we *do* have that end in sight. Our goal in writing this book is to call you to action. And the only action that will work here is collective action. We're not talking about a march on Washington, but a simple plan to embarrass the hell out of the politicians and bureaucrats perpetrating this outrage. So, read on knowing that your mounting rage will be put to perfect purpose.

CHAPTER 3

Welcome to Clawback Hell

I f the word "clawback" brings to mind a vicious image of an angry lobster or a mechanical hand, you're not alone! There is nothing gentle about the word. It's commonly used in corporate America to describe the demand for repayment of salary, bonus, and stock awards given to corporate executives who later have been found to have committed grievous errors in company management.

In fact, the term "clawback" was enshrined in securities law with the passage of the Sarbanes Oxley Act in 2002. That law specifically states:

> The Sarbanes-Oxley Act of 2002 includes a clawback provision, Section 304, which generally requires public company chief executive officers (CEOs) and chief financial officers (CFOs) to disgorge bonuses, other incentive- or equity-based compensation, and profits on sales of company stock that they receive within the 12-month period following the public release of financial information if there is a restatement because of material noncompliance, due to misconduct, with financial reporting requirements under the federal securities laws.

A clawback is, in other words, a punishment for misconduct in corporate America. And in that context, it is a meaningful response to bad judgment or outright lies or misleading information.

But in the case of Social Security, those who made the mistakes—the SS employees who calculate and determine and advise on benefits—are not punished. Instead, the innocent victims find their benefits being clawed back through no fault of their own.

Triple Checking Isn't Enough!

Even if you double- and triple-check with Social Security about your initial benefits amount, there is no way to be sure you're getting the correct payment unless, as discussed below, you keep careful track of your covered earnings, your non-covered pensions, and other relevant data and use MMSS or another meticulous benefit calculator. The consequences can be arbitrary and painful. Here's what one reader had to say about her experience:

> *Before I retired in 2015, I checked THREE times to be sure how much SS I would receive because I couldn't afford to retire without close budgeting. In August of 2018 I received a letter that I'd been overpaid by about $15,000 and my monthly benefit would be reduced to its "correct" amount.*

> *I appealed. I received a lesser SS payment but no decision about my appeal. In August of 2021 (3 years later) I received a letter saying I would receive $0 and that I would have to pay my Medicare out of pocket until my "debt" was repaid, approximately 2 years.*

> *Since then I have received $0 benefits, which had been in 2018 over $700/month AND have had to pay about $170/month for Medicare.*

Yes, you read that correctly. When Social Security demands its money back, it has all the power to reduce your future checks. Not only don't you receive payment, but if you were expecting your Medicare Part B premium to be deducted from your check, you might have to pay out of your own pocket since the clawback left nothing in your check.

The Social Security Run-Around

Here's a typical Social Security run-around story:

> I received a letter from Social Security in September 2022 stating that I owed them $20,500 for Medicare payments from 2020 to 2021. My Social Security was frozen. At that time, I was collecting on my husband's Social Security. Social Security received $104 in 2020 and $107 in 2021.
>
> They claim that I owe them for this money when I do not. I went to Social Security in October of 2022, and they had me fill out papers. They said that Social Security never checked my husband's record to see that that were getting the above amounts from him. They said it was their mistake, but Social Security had to fix it.
>
> They told me to call them back at the end of the month, which I did. When I called, they claimed they had no record of me coming in. I went back again to SS, and they told me the first lady did the wrong paperwork, and they had me fill out an appeal, which I did.
>
> I call each month to check on this and they keep telling me that Social Security hasn't looked at it yet. This is going on the 6th month. All they say is that they are too busy and understaffed. Can you please help me get back the $2500 that they took from me again (They took my Social Security money in November and December 2022). They have been paid twice for this! I would appreciate all help that I can receive.

Filing an Appeal

The Social Security website describes four steps to appealing one of these clawback letters. We explain them in detail in Chapter 20. They are:

- Request reconsideration. This process must be started within 60 days of receiving the notice. The request can be done online at https://www.ssa.gov/apply/appeal-decision-we-made/request-reconsideration. Or you can print out the form and mail/take it to your nearest Social Security office (which might require an appointment within the 60-day limit).

- Request a judicial hearing. You should receive a response to your reconsideration request, though many people report never hearing back. If you do get a response but disagree, you can request a hearing before a judge by filing online. But you must do so within 60 days of getting the answer to your initial appeal or forfeit all future rights. You may be represented by an attorney or other representative at this hearing.

- Request a review of hearing results. This must be done in writing, by filing Form HA 520.

- File a civil action against the government. This is the last resort, and it will be costly—if you can find an attorney to represent you, since these cases drag on. The costs could wipe out any eventual settlement. The case is filed in the U.S. District Court where you live.

One thing you should always keep in mind: Social Security sets deadlines for you; they do not keep deadlines for themselves. Your appeal and claims and request can drag on for years—during which time you may not receive the benefits you deserve.

Why You?

How does Social Security decide who to audit and when to file? Were you the winner of an unlucky lottery and your Social Security number came up? Social Security will only say that it audits benefits regularly and that audits may be triggered by new information about your income.

The closing of in-person office visits during the Covid epidemic worsened the information flow and the appeals process. There are several pending class actions alleging that during the pandemic Social

Security wrongly reduced benefits and made even its temporary simple waiver of penalties impossible to access, along with other agency decisions related to retirement, disability, and SSI payments.

But class-action suits move no more quickly than individual lawsuits. Both involve delays and legal fees. And that's not a solution to your immediate problem of getting the benefits you believe you deserve.

Don't Expect a Response

Social Security has all the power once you're in its sights. But don't expect a response. This email arrived in June 2023—a full year after the benefits stopped coming. How has this retired couple been living since they were notified?

> *I'd like to be included in your project against Social Security requesting payback money. They told my husband he owed $24,000 (out of the blue) and have stopped his benefits with no explanation. He submitted an appeal for explanation on 12.5.2022 and has yet to hear anything.*

Social Security is quick to stop payment when it wants to, but not quick to respond to your pleas for an explanation or help. Of course, that's not what the media department of Social Security says. In response to our question about situations like this, we received this statement from Social Security:

> "SSA does not recover the overpayment pending a decision on the request for an appeal or waiver. For more information, please refer to our publication at www.ssa.gov/pubs/EN-05-10098.pdf"

Guess it must have missed the appeal above, or dozens of others from people who claim they were clawed back even before they could request an appeal.

Time Is Money

Social Security takes its time dealing with these issues. And it has all the time in the world. But to a recipient, time is money. In fact, it appears that time is life to many seniors who are forced to do without their deserved benefits for many years. Until time runs out.

Antoinette wrote us a brief note with her plea for help:

> *Husband died in August 2020. Social Security deducted $475 in December 2020 from my benefit claiming overpayment. Filed appeal in October 2020 to get details on overpayment calculation. After several phone calls with Social Security since October 2020 promising a response, as of this date there has been no response from Social Security.*

Then her son wrote back a few weeks later, in June 2023, to say that Antoinette is now in hospice, so he further explained the situation on her behalf.

> *The appeal was filed to clarify the details. Several phone calls with different Social Security representatives from my mother with my sister were made to the local Social Security office. They confirmed receipt of the appeal and responded that another office processing the appeal had a backlog and would be notifying her shortly. It never happened. Due to my mother's declining health and the frustration of exceedingly long call wait times, contact with Social Security has not been made since late 2021.*

We brought this directly to the attention of Social Security and are hopeful that she will receive an answer and her money in her remaining time on earth.

Systems Disasters Abound

Why should innocent people have benefits withheld because of mistakes that Social Security acknowledges but simply cannot fix? And the situation worsens when Social Security must connect with another government agency, in this case the IRS.

If your 84-year-old parent or grandparent was dependent on a monthly check, how would you react to this story from Richard D?

This happened on my 2020 tax return. IRS accepted my return with $33,649.81 tax-exempt interest but reported to SS that it was $336,498.00.

SS's first letter to me was dated 11-7-2022 and I have received several other letters from them and transcripts they requested I get from IRS since then. I have met with Mr. Rameriz 3 times in the local SS office.

I met with Ms Kolp (ID#1000143496) in the local IRS office on 12-16-22. She agreed IRS was in error in reporting to SS, but she had to refer it to the IRS main office for them to contact Social Security. She also said there was a huge backlog of work and it would probably take several months before my problem is resolved. I did not ask for a letter acknowledging their mistake.

Meanwhile SS is withholding my monthly checks, plus I got a $63 monthly bill from Medicare starting this month. This is all due to IRS reporting a much higher income from my 2020 tax return.

Thank you so much for listening to my sad story. I sure would appreciate your help with this. I'm 84 years old and I hope I live to see this resolved.

The response to this issue from Social Security:

"We continue to expand data-matching agreements to help us ensure payment accuracy and eligibility."

Hopefully, that will be fast enough to get Richard his money in time for him to enjoy it.

Where's the Proof?

But what Social Security does *not* seem to owe any of the people from whom it demands a clawback is an accounting of how these amounts were calculated. We asked Social Security about the requirements for it to explain exactly how these clawback amounts were calculated. Its response:

> Overpayment notices include information about the payment amount the individual received and the payment amount the individual should have received for each month of the adjusted period; how and when the overpayment occurred; the individual's right to appeal; the individual's right to request a waiver of recovery of the overpayment; repayment options; and the need for the individual to contact us before we start collection efforts.

However, we have reviewed quite a few clawback letters. None provide any explanations, let alone proof that their alleged overpayment is correct. We also asked how the clawback accounts were discovered by Social Security. While not giving us a specific answer to the question, it seems that any new action (a request for widow's benefits, for example) would trigger a re-evaluation of prior benefits. But the errors may also be caught in routine analysis. As noted earlier, the process seems to be accelerating, with $8.6 billion added to the outstanding receivables in 2021 alone.

There was one bright note in the response from Social Security: They don't charge interest on the amount that must be repaid.

CHAPTER 4

Terrorizing Teachers and Other Public Servants

The Windfall Elimination Provision, or WEP, and the Government Pension Offset provision, or GPO, apply to people who work in government or other jobs from which Social Security FICA taxes are not withheld. The WEP is a formula used to reduce Social Security retirement benefits. The GPO reduces spousal benefits, divorced spousal benefits, widow(er)s benefits, and divorced widow(er) benefits received based on a current or former spouse's work record.

These adjustments are designed to make sure that non-covered workers, who might also qualify for Social Security benefits through other work or dependency, are treated no better or worse than anyone else. But both provisions are extremely crude adjustments, that in particular cases can be highly unfair.

Almost all workers in the noncovered sector are working for state or local governments that chose not to participate in Social Security. Some 7 million workers—roughly one-quarter of state and local government employees aren't covered by Social Security on their current job. Who are these workers? They are teachers, policemen, firemen, town clerks, city municipal workers, and, well, the list includes every type of worker employed by state and local governments.

But most workers in noncovered employment do spend some part of their working days in covered employment. If they spend long enough—long enough to accrue 40 credits, they can collect Social Security retirement benefits, based on their covered earnings.

Indeed, after 10 years of earning enough—above the so-called substantial earnings level (currently $29,700)—in covered employment, the WEP reduction is itself reduced as the worker spends more years earning above this level. After 30 years of covered work in jobs paying more than the substantial earnings level, the WEP reduction is zero.

Long story short, the WEP calculation is complicated. It depends critically on your covered earnings history, which Social Security may not get right. It also depends on any pensions you may receive from non-covered work as well as the amount of non-covered retirement account balances *at the time you start withdrawing from those accounts.*

Thus, you may have had two different careers in your lifetime, perhaps one as a corporate employee for many years and another as a teacher for a few years. Those few years in which Social Security was not deducted from your teaching paycheck, presumably because you were covered by a teacher's pension contribution, can have a huge impact on your eventual Social Security benefits.

If you *hadn't* become a teacher, but simply had the required 40 quarters of covered earned income in your corporate job, you would be eligible for your full Social Security retirement benefit, based on your highest 35 years of wage-indexed earnings. That's a pretty simple calculation.

WEP and GPO Reduce Social Security Benefits

Because you have even a small noncovered pension—paid by an employer that does not withhold Social Security taxes from your salary (typically, state and local governments or non-U.S. employers)—you are subject to the Windfall Elimination Provision. Yes, you contributed to Social Security in your corporate years, but the WEP means you won't get all those benefits you thought you earned. To repeat, the WEP benefit reduction applies unless you have at least 30 years of substantial earnings from which Social Security contributions were withheld.

The WEP reduces, but doesn't eliminate, your retirement benefit. *Your retirement benefit can't be reduced by more than half your non-*

covered pension. And, importantly, the WEP reduction in your Social Security benefit cannot take place until you start taking your noncovered pension.

If a public sector worker applies to claim the benefits earned by his or her private sector spouse, the GPO offset in the rule will reduce the amount of the monthly Social Security payment by two-thirds. That applies to spouses, surviving spouses, and even ex-spouses who might otherwise apply for Social Security benefits on the worker's account.

The GPO reduction impacts your retirement benefit before the WEP. It impacts your excess spousal, excess divorced spousal, excess widow(er)'s benefit, or excess divorced widow(er)'s benefit first. The GPO reduces these excess benefits by two-thirds of the worker's noncovered pension or imputed pension from a noncovered 403b pension. So, the GPO can wipe out your excess dependent benefit—even before the WEP reduction.

The WEP and GPO might both impact your Social Security benefit payment, depending on your situation.

If the WEP applies to you, you're not alone. According to Social Security, in 2020 the WEP applied to 3 percent of all beneficiaries (1.95 million beneficiaries out of 64.85 million total beneficiaries).

It applies to Ann. And it severely impacts her retirement benefits:

I am a retired teacher in Illinois. I receive a pension from TRS. During my teaching years I worked summer jobs in which I paid into SS. If I didn't have a pension, I would be entitled to $687 a month on my record. Because of the penalty of having a pension I will not receive this.

And to make matters worse, my husband died in December 2021 and I do not get any SS payments from his record. I hope your research helps to eliminate the WEP and GPO restrictions on SS.

If you think the WEP is unfair, you're also not alone. The Social Security Fairness Act to eliminate both the WEP and the GPO has strong bipartisan support in Congress. But unless the WEP is elimi-nated, your Social Security benefits will be permanently reduced.

We have tried to make this a simple explanation. But, of course, you want to know the specifics. For that, here's the explanation of the WEP reduction taken straight from the Social Security website.

How the WEP Works

Social Security benefits are calculated by applying three different percentages to a person's lifetime average indexed monthly earnings (AIME) and adding them up to obtain the worker's monthly benefit (primary insurance amount (PIA)) at full retirement age. For most beneficiaries in 2022, the PIA equals the sum of:

- 90 percent of the first $1,024 of AIME, plus
- 32 percent of AIME over $1,024 and through $6,172, plus
- 15 percent of AIME over $6,172.

The WEP PIA replicates the regular PIA but scales down the first percentage from 90 percent to 40 percent in increments of five percentage points for workers with less than 30 years of coverage (YOCs). Thus, workers with 30 or more YOCs have a first PIA factor of 90 percent, workers with 21–29 YOCs have a first PIA factor between 45–85 percent, and workers with 20 YOCs have a first PIA factor of 40 percent.

However, the difference between the regular PIA and the WEP PIA cannot exceed one-half of the monthly noncovered pension. This provision is known as the WEP guarantee and results in a smaller WEP reduction to the Social Security benefit than otherwise would have applied.

Because these computations are too complex for many of us, we leave it to the representatives at Social Security to work it out on their super-computers to give us the correct benefit amount.

And that is where disaster starts—and future clawbacks are born.

Calculating the WEP Reduction

The WEP reduction is complicated. Add in the issue of the GPO offset, and spousal benefits, and the resulting reduced benefit often comes as a shock. Here's a horror story from Donna to illustrate that surprise:

> *I am a 64-year-old woman who, prior to 2014 was extremely healthy and independent, despite my husband's early death in 2005. In 2014 I had an emergency brain surgery, which left me extremely compromised. I have a multitude of problems that have taken away a lot of my independence.*
>
> *Due to the surgery I was unable to go back to work full-time as a school counselor. I have been living off a disability pension I receive from TRS for several years now, plus my own Social Security, which of course was cut by 2/3 per the government.*
>
> *This year I looked into taking my husband's Social Security, albeit early but necessary. I was quite shocked to learn that because I had worked in the school system, my deceased husband's Social Security would also be cut by 2/3, because I am the recipient I guess.*
>
> *I felt very angry about this, for he had worked many years at a very demanding job, I was more angry that they were taking money from him than I was about not receiving his full award. I still am angry. I feel it is very unfair, and no one can tell me where his money will actually go, since I am not going to be the recipient of it, nor will he, of course.*

Whose Money Is It?

The last line of Donna's letter illustrates an issue that doesn't receive much public discussion. There's a sense that you have an "account" at Social Security into which you—and your employer—paid contributions over the years. True old-timers will remember the term "a shoebox in Maryland," which was popularly used to describe the money Social Security—then based in Maryland—was collecting on your behalf.

Today we know there is no such separate account. And on the plus side, we also know that even noncontributing spouses (and ex-spouses if married for 10 years and not remarried) can collect benefits on your account. As well, minor children do collect benefits on the Social Security accounts of deceased or disabled parents. And some minor children even collect benefits just because their parent has reached full retirement age and started to collect his or her own benefits.

But if you die earlier than projected, there is no refund for the unpaid amounts that were collected in your name. And because of the WEP and GPO offsets described above, there may be reductions in your benefits—despite the fact that you paid in to the Trust Fund over the years.

The bottom line for Social Security is that some families do come out far ahead of what they contributed. And because of death or these arcane offsets, some families are deprived of the full benefits they thought they would receive.

If you work in an uncovered job, you should know that despite paying into Social Security in other years, your benefits will be substantially reduced. And, as mentioned above, if there ever is a Social Security reform bill, it's likely that the WEP offset will be addressed. In the meantime, you should be aware of the WEP—not only when it comes time to take benefits, but when you consider the impact of a job change.

Clawbacks Because of WEP

By far, the greatest number of clawback complaints we have received revolve around the WEP. Not the unfairness of the WEP itself, but the initial incorrect calculations made by Social Security personnel when benefits involve a WEP reduction.

Let's be clear. We have *not* received even one complaint from individuals who can document that they are being *under*paid in their monthly benefit check because of the WEP. How could the ordinary retiree figure that out anyway, given the formula above? Most grudgingly accept the benefit calculations of Social Security.

No. The WEP clawback horror stories revolve around alleged *over*payments—repayment demands from Social Security because of its initial incorrect calculations of benefits using this complicated formula. Now, suddenly, and years later, Social Security wants its money back!

As you read the following two stories, it becomes clear that not only did Social Security make initial mistakes, but it is not willing to explain or justify its new calculations that result in the clawbacks. If Social Security couldn't get the calculations right in the first place, why should we believe it is doing a better job now?

That's the question that Maggie is asking as a result of the interaction between her county pension and spousal benefits from her deceased husband:

> *I am one of the people who received a letter few months ago regarding overpayment .I am receiving pension from the county and Social security from my deceased husband. I haven't received any money from my husband's Social Security for the last 6 months. I was told that I owe them so they are not sending my monthly check until they collected what I owe who knows till when. I was calling them and [they were] giving me different answers. I don't really understand how these things happened. I hope you can help us regarding this matter.*

While Maggie really doesn't understand the system, Sue has another view. Sue actually *did* repay $9,000 to Social Security, and now it is demanding more:

> *I too, have been a victim of Social Security wanting me to pay them money that they said I have been over paid. Before Covid I paid them back $9,000. And I think I legitimately was overpaid, because I retired that year but worked until August. But since last summer they have said that I owe them an additional $5000.*

I have filled out all the paperwork disputing this and have gone to the Social Security office two times and several hours of phone conversations. Each time I've requested a printout of what I've paid, what they've paid me, what figure was allowed to be paid to me, so I could actually do the math and see it in black-and-white. Each time I was promised that the printout would be sent to me, but I never have received it.

My benefits [have] now ended. I only receive $300 a month, because I have a teacher pension, but my teacher pension is not that large, because I came into education later in life as a teacher. The $300 a month in my case is a lot of money. Anything that you can do to shed some light on the situation so that I can pursue it further would be most appreciated.

Social Security will demand—and take—your money any way it can get it. If you pay the requested money back, it can demand more. It can reduce your benefits arbitrarily, leaving you little to live on in retirement.

Who's to Blame?

When Social Security makes a mistake calculating the WEP, it's not always— as it claims—because people didn't provide the correct documentation. But since Social Security calculates the benefit, few people would be aware of an error in calculations. Here's what happened to Emily:

By their own admission, they entered my public school pension as a one-time payment instead of a monthly benefit. Eight years ago. At one time, they cut off my SS and Medicare entirely. I filed an appeal about two years ago, but received no response, except to say they had received the appeal.

Now they're threatening me again. I would have to sell my house to repay their mistake. My (deceased, 20 years ago) husband and I paid into SS for over 60 years total. Absolutely maddening, and I seem to have no recourse!!!

Emily faces triple-whammy Social Security error. It miscalculated her benefits. Then it cut off all her benefits despite acknowledging that it received her appeal. And it never scheduled a hearing.

Despite no hearing, her benefits were briefly restored. Now Social Security is demanding repayment again—still without ever acknowledging her appeal.

Can you imagine having this threat hanging over your head many years into retirement—and on your own, depending on a small pension and minimal Social Security because of the WEP?

CHAPTER 5

Impoverishing the Disabled

I f you are disabled, you are almost surely living hand to mouth. But you likely worked and paid into Social Security, making you and your dependents eligible for a lifeline—Social Security benefits. This lifeline can easily be cut from one day to the next via a clawback letter.

The Social Security Disability Program became law in 1956, under President Eisenhower. At the time, there was great debate about whether the program would be abused by those claiming to be disabled.

As a result, the initial disability program paid benefits only to those age 50 and older. But as the disability program expanded over the years and was joined by the Supplemental Security Income program in 1975, the financial impact on the Trust Funds became difficult to ignore.

These programs were created by Congress, and any changes to them must be legislated by Congress. It is up to the employees of the Social Security Administration to follow the complex rules in distributing the benefits that have been legislated. And that is no easy task when significant money is being handed out.

There is an all-too-obvious incentive to cheat the system. You may have seen stories about people cheating on their disability applications—caught on TV by local news crews, playing golf when they said they couldn't even stand up to go to work. That's why Social Security reviews disability applications, checks medical records, and does its best to weed out malingerers. It's a stringent process, resulting in long delays.

The Realities of Disabilities Claims

The Social Security website says approval for disability takes from three to five months for processing applications. But the reality is that Social Security does not have any deadline for making those decisions. In fact, an entire cottage industry of attorneys has sprung up to advise people on filing disability claims and appealing denials.

In December 2022, the SSA approved a little fewer than one in five first-time applicants. Most people must appeal their initial denials, especially if they don't have a lawyer handling their cases. That process could take as long as three years. Only in terminal cases, such as advanced cancer, is there a chance for fast-track approval.

And, once approved, disability checks do not start until the sixth month after approval. So, whether you applaud Social Security's diligence in paying benefits or are appalled by the delays, this is certainly no easy process. Of necessity, it involves subjective decisions. And because of complexity, it invites computational errors.

But none of those issues absolves Social Security of blame for its errors, or responsibility for the manner in which it treats applicants and clients. The simple fact is that most people who file for disability and receive it assume Social Security knows what it's doing when it sends out their checks.

Like Rhonda:

I'm one of many being told I've got an overpayment from the Social Security administration. It's stemming from the time frame talked about in your article. This was when Covid-19 was at its height. Now their demanding I return some $27,000 to them and I'm at a loss as to why. I collect disability for mental health issues but I did work p/t and f/t but it was all reported to them, so why are they coming back at me now with this?

Good question, Rhonda.

Disability Mistakes

Anyone receiving SSDI income has been through tough times—first in losing the ability to do gainful work (as described by the statute) and then by the process of applying for disability benefits.

Now, imagine what it would feel like if—after all this initial process—Social Security contacts you some years later and says it made a mistake. You don't qualify, after all. And it wants its money back. A lot of money.

You don't have to imagine. All you have to do is read this email, printed in its entirety and without editing, (as are all the emails in our book) to feel the pain of a family going through this process.

Ms Savage—I hope I'm starting off correctly! FINALLY someone wants to hear, and possibly help, with my horror story about overpayment (I've come to detest this word!) by Social Security. I am a 62yr old grmom, widow for almost 2 yrs, and raising our 2 grkids who we adopted in 2011. They are now 15 and 17.

I get disability, since 2018, and widows benefits. Kids get survivors benefits. My husband made very good money, working on power plants, insulation and sheet metal work during shut downs. But he fell in 2003, imploding his spinal cord. Was told he'd never walk again but him being the man he was he was taking baby steps his 3rd day! After a stay in hospital then rehabilitation he applied for disability. In meantime, he began getting his workers compensation. Got approved for disability so was getting paid from both.

Things rocked on normally for years until somewhere about 2015 or 2016 (forgive me, my memory not what it use to be). He received the letter stating he has been overpaid by social security. He made several calls to find out what the hell only to be given run around.

Finally someone told him computer error, forget about it. So we did. Whew! Then he was diagnosed with esophageal cancer. Had surgery. Couldn't get it. He passed away April 2021.

At some point I applied for our survivors benefits and approved. Then it started again, letters about overpayments to kids. For what? Up until last week nobody would answer that. She said he never told about his workers comp so his disability wasn't figured with offset.

We'll be damn sure did! We took even more than was necessary papers and forms and info when he has his interview. They sent me form to fill out for a waiver so no money be held out yet. . . . YET. It got denied.

But a couple or 3 months went by and I didn't hear anything. Then another letter stating the next month they would be holding both kids checks. . . . ALL of it! And they did!

Each one of their checks is more than my 2 lil checks together. It sunk me. I had just gotten my credit cleaned up, credit score was almost excellent, some money saved, and yes we lived well. I ended up having to let my credit cards go to collections, some judgements.

Makes my stomach turn. I got behind on everything. Going to food pantries (thank God for them). But I did it. We made it and still had our home (which got paid off in Jan!!) And our vehicles and food on the table.

Then it happened again. March 3 I checked bank . . . this is our payday. Nope. Just my checks deposited, not kids. I called them. On hold for an hour only to have the person who answered tell me I called the wrong SS # and she hung up.

Called other #, after 20min on hold this lady told me there's nothing she can do. The overpayment happened and they will hold kids checks 2 months a year. I told her I had set up payments a couple weeks ago. (Forgot to mention that call! She said I did not. It's not in computer.

Well I damn sure did, $360 each kid every month. No ma'am, whole check, each. Said last papers I sent back with my receipts and spending showed that I'm not strapped. My bills aren't that much. I was shocked. But bit my lip cuz after all she has our future in her hands.

Now I'm facing insurance lapsing, electric ($647!!) being shut off, have a car in the shop that I can't fix now, and don't have any pennies to pinch. During all this, not only did I lose my hubby but my dad also passed away. My daughter got into some legal trouble, I was sunk in depression causing me to procrastinate to a fault. I had a heart attack. And now can't afford the gas to go to cardiologist for check up.

Horror story? I think so. . . . I can't believe with the way prices are sky rocketing, SS thinks it's ok to withhold ALL of their monies! How is this legal? I don't mind paying back if they prove I (kids) really owe it but they haven't done that. I have to figure out something and fast!

My apologies if this was too long!!"

What's behind this situation? When Social Security calculates disability payments, it is supposed to take workers' comp benefits into account. Did that happen in this case? The widow says they showed their entire financial picture. And they started receiving benefits.

Her husband's death triggered the recalculation of benefits, revealing Social Security's mistake—years later.

It's bad enough to learn that the government wants its money back from you. The situation is overwhelming when the government won't communicate. Our writer was fearful of disclosing her full name, cowed by the power of the government. And here's why:

- They never documented the reason for the clawback.
- They never acknowledged her payment plan in writing.
- They arbitrarily decided to withhold two checks per year—as opposed to acknowledging her repayment plan.
- She submitted receipts for her living expenses, and was told she was too comfortable ("not strapped" enough) to receive benefits—with no explanation of any income/spending limits on survivors benefits.

Can you blame her for her fear of what might come next?

Social Security's Record-keeping Mess

In reviewing the many sad stories sent to us by people who have had disability benefits clawed back, one of the most startling factors is not the initial miscalculations, but how long it takes Social Security to adjust its payments—based on work records reported by the beneficiaries in an attempt to make sure that their efforts to return to work do not come back to haunt them.

It's clearly up to Social Security to modify the disbursements based on what the recipient reports. But even when best efforts are made, Social Security gets it wrong. In the story that follows, Kathleen became disabled on October 25, 2013 and her disability payments started in April, 2014.

Her husband, Tim, reports that when Kathleen made an effort to get back to work in February 2015, she notified SSA by phone that she was back to work. And the checks kept coming, so this family felt they were within Social Security's period of transition, quoting the website policy statement:

> "After a person becomes eligible for disability benefits, the person may attempt to return to the work force. As an incentive, we provide trial work period in which a beneficiary may have earnings and still collect benefits."

Imagine their shock when they received a bill for $37,043.90. Making it worse, Social Security listed two different dates for the overpayment period. A lawyer declined to help them appeal on the grounds there was "no way to fight city hall." So, they are now in the process of repaying the overage at the rate of $100 per month—hoping it won't impact their eventual Social Security retirement benefits.

Tim stressed that they just assumed, after notifying Social Security, that Social Security knew what it was doing in continuing to send benefits, while his wife attempted to work while undergoing chemo and surgeries.

> *The key here, in my opinion, is that they knew Kathleen was back at work and continued to send payments for months afterward. We did not know that we were not entitled to these payments and so continued to cash the checks and use the money toward considerable healthcare bills and other vital expenses. Who would collect these checks and put them aside "just in case?"*

> *Why the considerable delay between them knowing about the work, determining that she was not entitled to benefits, and yet continuing to send benefits? In this day and age of advanced systems and instant communication, those payments should have been stopped immediately, or at the very least within a month or two. Yet here we are paying for their considerable inefficiencies. Our government is supposed to help its citizens, not hunt them down and demand compensation for mistakes that they make.*

Returning to Work with Disability

The clawback of disability benefits is due partly to the complexity of the regulations and partly to the changing nature of work opportunities for the disabled. For those who truly want to work, there are income limits that must be watched for fear of losing benefits. And, as you'll see in the story below, there is little flexibility for those who make even the smallest misstep.

I've been on SSDI since about 2011 due to severe mental illness and resulting treatment causing severe short-term memory issues. Initially I was unable to work but since 2014 I have worked part-time. In 2015 I tried the Ticket to Work program working full-time but could not master the necessary tasks to keep employment in that environment (previously I had been a Clinical Project Manager in the Pharmaceutical Research Industry). I had SSDI reviews in 2019, 2021 and I believe 2022. (I also tried the Ticket to work program again in 2021—as it had been over 5 years since I had previously tried it—again with disastrous results for my health).

On 3/25/2023 I received a notice from Social Security that on 8/2019 I had made $81 over SGA and my disability was being discontinued immediately and I owed them $61,000+. The same day my ex-husband (whom I live with along with our disabled son) received the same letter from the SSA stating that our son (who has autism, mental retardation and hearing impairment) was also being kicked off of his SSI program due to ME working $81 over SGA in 8/2019 and he owes $30,000+.

No one in the Social Security Administration can explain to me why my 27 year old son was kicked off due to MY work record with Social Security when his SSI program was approved under his own name, social security number, and with his father as his representative payee. Never mind the fact that I had SSDI reviews since 2019 which continued my disability.

I only made $8,000 in 2019—so I clearly wasn't making over SGA in any one month. It is possible that it was a 3 paycheck month—but I shouldn't be penalized for that. I wasn't working a ton of hours or making a lot of money.

So here we sit—on the verge of homelessness because our family lost approximately $2,000 of our monthly income *with no notice. We are not supposed to pick up extra hours at our work (I work 20 hours a week at a retirement community) because SSA is still making a decision on us, yet we cannot afford to pay our bills, put food on the table and a roof over our head. We have appealed the decision and the $91,000+ bill that goes along with it (I think the bank statements I submitted in person to the Woodridge, IL SSA office showed at that time I had a balance of $-54.90 in my bank account.*

Whatever you can do to help me and the other families like ours who are being terrorized by the SSA would be great.

If you're starting to notice a pattern, you'd be right. Not only does Social Security manage to find the weakest, poorest, and most disabled recipients to audit and file claims against. It clearly becomes less respectful and more arbitrary as soon as it realizes how powerless the victim is.

This horror story came from James who exposes the darkest, most cruel side of the Social Security bureaucracy.

My 60-year-old brother-in-law is special needs. He is a poster child for the Reagan reforms in that though he can not read he has maintained a job at Home Depot for decades attending to the lot.

In 1998 his mother, with whom he lived until her death in 2021, began receiving financial assistance from SS on behalf of her son. She was a widow at the time and he was earning a minimum wage job. But that year Home Depot hired him and his wages increased. His mother was concerned and went to the local SS office and was told not to worry about it. So for the years 1998 -2002 the assistance checks arrived monthly. Then the letter came stating that the overpayments needed to be paid back to the amount close to $30,000! His wages had exceeded the floor for assistance.

Now my mother-in-law had led a difficult life after losing her husband at a young age. She raised four children on wages as a Union Clerk. Always living hand to mouth the extra SS funds for her disabled son went a long way each month. But now the letters started warning her of the consequences if she did not pay it back.

So arrangements were made to begin to pay what she could afford, which amounted to $30 per month. She paid this until the day she passed away. However $28,620 remained on the due ledger so of course SS turned to the special needs son for repayment. Mind you he had no idea of any of this as his mother was the one who received the funds.

So on June 7th, 2021 my wife wrote SS a letter which had over 40 pages of attachments explaining the situation and letting them know her mother had passed on. Her special needs brother had moved in with another brother as he would be unable to live alone and keep up with the cost of living. She requested a waiver of overpayment based on all of the facts and included wage summaries and a detailed doctors diagnosis of her brothers functional capacities. On December 20th, 2021 she received a reply that they had received the request and would respond to it.

On December 16th, 2022 she received a letter demanding payment and had never heard back as to the status of her request. This was the last correspondence she received on this matter which is obviously still pending soon to be two years since she requested the waiver.

If the SS administration were to claw back from his wages it would be grossly unfair to him. I am proud to call him my brother-in-law and had for years admired the tenacity with which he overcome obstacles in his life. Over the years he worked with special instructors in order to obtain his drivers license even though he can not read. This opened up further freedoms for him and his work has given him pride in his ability to sustain his living. Like his mother however he and his brother live month to month with the ever rising cost of living.

In summary we have found the SS department to be cold and unresponsive. No one obviously cares about the humanity in a situation like this, only what the regulations say to do.

We will keep you informed if they come after him in the future. We hope that this history along with the others you are collecting can spur action for reform in this government entity. Should you need any additional details for your files please let me know and I will be happy to provide.

This seems to be a good place to stop and once again post the motto of Social Security, proudly proclaimed on its website:

"We are passionate about supporting our customers by delivering financial support, providing superior customer service, and ensuring the safety and security of your information."

Well, it may be passionate about information security—but not quite so concerned about information processing. The impact of this systemic failing is clear in the story of Tim and Kathleen, above.

The simple fact is that not only has Social Security fallen behind in dealing with important current information. Its computer systems are a mess, as Sarah clearly explains below:

The paperwork from SSA will blow your mind. Dollar amounts changing months in their system. Computers don't do that on their own. Statements that are clearly designed to baffle and confuse a disabled person. Multiple statements days apart that conflict each other so that no one has any clue what is going on or will go on.

I even received two 1099s one year 4 days apart with different amounts. The original lady that worked on the overpayment has retired and no one could make heads or tails of her notes. She gave me over $14,000 back via check and then the new people under the authority of Supervisor Ms. Webster in the Cleburne, Texas office demanded it back.

It was an SSA Representative that informed me of regulation 404.1028. I researched and read social security regulations over and over. If it doesn't count as employment then it shouldn't count as wages so nothing to report. It's an allowed exemption under SSA regulations.

I wasn't trying to steal or get anything I shouldn't have. I had multiple failed work attempts but continued to do my best to return to employment. I wasn't sitting on my ass collecting a check. I put myself through severe distress and hardship to do all I could to be a responsible citizen not a moocher.

For this, I'm penalized repeatedly and terrorized with the fear of losing my check every month since 2016. This has only made my disability worse . . . my suffering worse.

In my opinion, this is also exploitation which is a crime. They've withheld my money illegally. There's zero transparency. There's no accountability. Office of Inspector General has been contacted repeatedly and no resolution to date. Blackmailed in 2021 by SSA in which they took $300/ month for 6 months. I didn't agree. I signed nothing. I asked for 1099s for appeals and they refused. Threatened to withhold my entire check unless I gave up all rights to appeals and tried to force me into saying it was my debt. I did not agree. I did not sign. They still took my money then too. Like I said, complicated but documented.

Notice that Sarah was explicit about her efforts to get back to work. She's not alone in that desire. Were you tempted to think that all these claimants were the ones who had made mistakes? Are you contemplating the possibility that they got on a gravy train of monthly payments and made no effort to be honest about their situation? Well, think again!

Time after time, the emails we received explain their extreme efforts to contact Social Security, to update a work situation, to acknowledge income from work. But it all goes into a void—until the lottery machine that is Social Security spits out your number. Then it comes after you, never acknowledging your efforts to stay in its good graces.

That's what happened to Nancy:

Dear Terry,

My SS story is turning into a horror story, leaving me wondering how I'm going to manage to live after I can no longer work. I'm only 55 so I have lots of years left to work.

I applied for SSDI in 2011 because of a chronic illness which caused extreme pain. My ex-husband and I split up in 2015 and I was lucky enough to find a remote, part-time job that allowed me to set the hours that I worked and I did my best to stay under the limit that SS says I could earn monthly without affecting my benefits.

In 2019, I was notified that I'd made more money than was permitted and that I wouldn't be able to receive benefits until it was paid back. It was about $16,000. In March of 2020, I was informed that I would begin receiving benefits again.

I was able to find a full time remote job in April of 2021. At that point, I called my local Social Security to have the payments stopped and then contacted Medicare to the same.

In 2022, I received a letter from SSA informing me that they'd overpaid me and I owe them $51,000. I called and was told how to file an appeal, which I did and never received a response.

I received another letter on May 27th of this year informing me that now I owe them $61,000. They can't explain how that happened and want me to bear the responsibility of proving that I don't. I don't want to lose my house or pay the government back until the day I die! I don't know what to do anymore.

Stop and take a deep breath. Imagine yourself, or your sister, or your mother, caught up in this situation: Trying to rebuild a life after illness and divorce, trying to honestly report your current status to Social Security, and trying to build retirement income through earned Social Security benefits. Then receiving a bill from Social Security saying it had made a mistake and that you were overpaid by $61,000.

And, by the way, how could that amount jump by $10,000 in one year?

The Most Disabled Lose the Most

Mimi's lifelong disability sentence has followed her into old age. Her total disability should have been converted to monthly retirement benefits. But once again, Social Security's massive records failure and total indifference have further destroyed a life:

Hello, I am a disabled person who has been on Social Security since I became an adult until 1993 at which point I got a GED and went to college I got off of Social Security and went to work. In the year 2000 I was hit by a drunk driver and injured by the year 2005. I realized I couldn't successfully work anymore and I got back on disability payments.

When I turned 65 I received a letter stating I no longer disabled. I'm now retired, and then I need to go to work to earn the points that I need to have part A and B for my Medicare.

I've had three appointments with Social Security to where <u>they told me they have absolutely no record of me being declared, totally disabled by Judge Shore in San Francisco in 1977.</u>

They also say they have no record of me being on Social Security from 1977 until 1993. They do have a record that I didn't work all that time.

I can't figure it out. Oh and the third appointment they just didn't show up for it. It was a phone appointment during coronavirus and they never called. I've gone to the disability attorneys referred me to someone else who's called me, but then hung up on me after I told him what I'm calling about and I can't seem to get any relief. My medical bills are out of pocket because of this.

The program that was designed by Congress to create a safety net has instead ensnared those least able to make themselves heard.

Arbitrary? Mean-spirited? Devastating? Have we lost our ability to be outraged? We think not. And that is why we call on the Social Security Administration to set up a special task force to modernize the disability insurance program by setting up a new computerized documentation that interfaces with the IRS to record income paid to disabled persons.

And we request a higher-level review, along with a documented sign-off for clawbacks from disabled recipients. Surely that's not too much to ask of an agency that is "passionate about delivering financial support and giving superior customer service."

CHAPTER 6

The Claw from the Grave

They say the sins of the fathers shall not be put upon the sons, but apparently Social Security hasn't gotten this biblical message. [Deuteronomy 24:16] But even in death, you may not be able to escape the dreaded Social Security clawback reaching into your pocket. Or at least the concern that your problems will one day fall on your children. The irony is that we ask our children to pay into the system that destroys their parents' financial security.

Just to put things in perspective, here's Tamara's intergenerational Social Security horror story just as she sent it to us. It's a long story but it demonstrates so much of what needs to be fixed about the Social Security system.

It shows you exactly how arbitrary the clawback demands from Social Security are—and the lengths the agency will go to collect—45 years! It shows clearly that Social Security cannot document the reasons or the amounts it claims must be repaid. This story also demonstrates how unreachable the agency is, and how sloppily it keeps records, and loses them. It demonstrates that even agreements for reduced payments are never put on file in individual records, and why the same demands resume out of the blue when all was thought settled.

I've been dealing with this problem for about 2 years. It concerns my 80 yr old mother's SS checks . . . and your story now has me worried that this may haunt my sister and I unless we can get it resolved.

*A couple yrs ago, my mother received a letter from SS . . .
saying that they believed she was overpaid approx $6000 . . .
about 45 yrs ago.*

*She was a young widow, and my sister and I were eligible to
collect benefits from our father's SS starting in approx 1977.
I was about 14 when my father died of cancer. . . . My mother
had worked part-time for several years prior to his death . . .
and she continued to do so.*

*I remember her telling me that when she spoke to the man at
social security office, he said he would divide the amount we
were eligible to receive, into 3 checks each month. . . . One to my
mother, one to my mother for me and one to my mother for my
sister. She told the man she planned to continue working, but he
seemed to believe she wouldn't and said that he would just set
it up so her name was already in the system . . . and if she quit
working, it would be easier to add her benefit to the amount.*

*I have heard that explanation several times over the years . . .
as to why she got a check in her name. So she did continue to
work . . . and remarried a few yrs later. My sister and I both
continued to receive checks in our own name after we turned
18 while we continued to take college classes. When we stopped
going to college the checks stopped.*

*Many years go by. My mother continued to work off and on
over the next 30 odd years. Eventually she decided to collect
her own social security at age 66, I believe. She collected her
approximately $980 social security for 12-13 years.*

*Now, the SS administration believes she was overpaid, 45 yrs
ago and says she owes nearly $6000. The first letter said they
would be keeping her entire check for the next 7 months unless
she filled out a certain form, claiming she didn't believe she
owed the money, because it wasn't her fault, or paying it back
would cause undue hardship.*

She made several calls to get an appointment at the social security office in Lake Mary Florida, but this was during the covid pandemic, and everything had to be submitted electronically or left in the drop box. She wrote a letter explaining that she did not believe she was overpaid . . . but due to it being 45 years ago, she has no paperwork that gives details of what the benefit amount was supposed to be, or whether that amount included a widow benefit, or was just for the children.

We have never been shown any paperwork from SS that proves how they came to this conclusion . . . and we have no way at this late date to argue her case.

Eventually, after filling out forms it was concluded that she hadn't proved that she did not owe the money . . . but since her monthly check is her only source of income, SS agreed in a follow up letter, to take $51 dollars a month, for several years until the $6000 was paid back.

Her checks continued to arrive, minus the $51. Until the beginning of the following year, when she again received a letter stating the exact same thing; that she owed thousands of dollars, and the SS administration was going to keep all her entire check for several months until they were paid back!

At this point the Lake Mary FL branch office had reopened, and we went in and talked to someone in person, thinking surely this would be an easy fix . . . but again, forms were filled out, nobody could explain why they weren't honoring the letter they send the previous year stating that $51 a month would be collected for the next several years.

After several trips to speak to people in person, we finally got a supervisor that reinstated the original agreement—but my 81 yr old mother swears to this day she doesn't owe it. But she has no way to fight it and has not seen any evidence that she actually does. . . . She is constantly terrified that her check will one day just stop showing up . . . and she needs that money desperately . . . as I said, it is her only source of income. And my step father is in the same boat, with his health quickly deteriorating.

As I am now 61, and getting closer to considering when to begin collecting my SS check . . . after reading your article about the poor man in Michigan, being forced to pay back $ his mother collected. . . . I wonder if the same is apt to happen to me, should my mother die before its all paid back.

Yes, Social Security can impact generations arbitrarily. That goes against even the laws of bankruptcy and probate. In both courts, unsecured debts owed by a bankruptcy claimant or the deceased cannot be held against the individual's relatives.

If you declare bankruptcy and list your credit card balances, your creditors cannot come after you after your debts have been discharged. If you die with a mortgage on your home, the bank can demand repayment or sell the home and recoup their secured loan.

We do not have debtor's prisons in the United States. We allow unsecured debts to die with the individual. Obviously, Social Security plays by its own rules. It can and will come after you for your parents' behavior—even after they are dead and buried. It's an example of the unchecked use of its power.

Generation after Generation Must Pay

Here's a claw-from-the-grave story where the writer asked us not to use their family names, out of fear of further reprisals from Social Security.

My brother received Social Security disability payments for one year. It was not enough to live on so he went back to work. Social Security did not stop payments. My brother succumbed to poor health and passed away while trying to pay back SS with nominal payments.

*Now Social Security has passed the remaining $19,000
balance owed to my sister-in-law. She appealed the
overpayment 4 times since my brother debt resulting in 4
denials. She survives on only her SS payments with no other
assets. SS will now begin deducting $500 monthly until debt
is paid!!!*

*How can SS transfer debt to spouse who has no assets? Can
an attorney be of any help?*

Imagine your family subjected to this kind of harassment. It's a revealing look inside Social Security and the people who work there.

Young and Abused by SSA for Parents' Long-Ago Claims

We have uncovered many horror stories of children who were minors at the time their parents received benefits on their behalf. And now that they are young adults, they learn from Social Security that the agency wants its money back—from them!

This typically happens when a parent is retired, disabled, or deceased. Surviving minor children are entitled to benefits on the parent's work record, as are children under 18, or 19 if still in school. Or benefits may be given when a low-income parent claims Supplemental Security Income (SSI) benefits for a child. Despite the number of children in the family, the maximum family Social Security benefit ranges from 150 percent to 180 percent of the original payee's benefit.

This letter from Jacob puts the issue in a nutshell, or should we say in a SS "nut-case." This long and detailed description of benefits given to a parent for a five-year-old child—then being clawed back as soon as that child entered the workforce—is as grotesque as a horror story could be.

*I heard you were collecting social security horror stories. So I
figured I'd throw you mine.*

I received a letter from social security back in 2019, when I was 20, saying that I owed them $12,163. And that I had 60 days to pay them, or else.

I was a college student working a retail job and living with family. Family which did not have the resources to help pay for any legal aid that this threatening letter might require.

I will spare you the exact details of how things played out. I honestly don't remember most of them clearly. But fast forward through a bunch of stress, research, confusion, panic, more confusion and more stress.

I found out that my mother, who I was living with at the time of the "overpayment," had received a large lump sum from social security when my dad finally won his case for disability. When that happens benefits are paid out going back to the date the disability claim was first filed.

Apparently Social Security has a benefit for the children of disabled workers, which my mother was and my dad became. So as their child "I" received a benefit for being their child, as they were disabled. Which they gave directly to my mother to spend. And which I was never informed of and knew nothing about.

We'll actually I knew a little about it. See I knew my mother received money for me living there, a teenager is capable of figuring out that much, but I had no idea it was "my" money from "my" benefit. I assumed that she got money monthly for having a dependent minor while being disabled. So that it was hers, her benefit, for her being disabled and having a child. She did whatever paperwork to get the money, got the money put directly in her bank account, and got to spend it however she deems appropriate. That's how other government benefits involving children work.

Makes sense right? Well Social Security doesn't think so. Instead, they claim it was MY benefit.

See, it says it right there, in the 700 page policy handbook. It's your benefit, your parent is just the representative payee. And we need a representative payee because obviously child you can't be expected to know anything about money.

Oh, but you are both, parent and child, equally liable for paying back any overpayments.

This arrangement only makes sense in the Byzantine world of administrative law.

To anyone of sound mind, this logic is clearly contradictory, deeply immoral, and working against the goal of having these benefits exist in the first place.

It is clearly the disabled parents benefit for having the child, and not the child's benefit for having disabled parents.

If you have to appoint a representative payee for someone because they don't have the competence to be given the money directly, you cannot hold them responsible for paying any of it back if there's an overpayment. Can you??

At the time when I first received social security's extortion letter, my mother was still alive. Unfortunately for social security you cannot squeeze blood from a stone, or money from the disabled poor. So I assume, rather than go after her for it, they waited till I was an adult; so they could come after me for it.

I called social security, tried to figure out the situation, and asked them to send me a breakdown of the overpayment and why I am legally obligated to pay it back.

They should be able to show both of those things, how else would they know how much I owe or that I even owe it? They chose to just never send me anything I ever asked for. The only letters I got from them was the ones telling me my tax refunds have been taken by them for the delinquent debt owed to them.

Well, at least I knew they had my current address!

After doing more and more research and feeling more and more helpless, I gave up. I figured if that's all they were going to do I'd just let them. And I'd just plan around never actually getting any tax returns.

Well Social security would appropriate my tax returns one year to put towards the "debt", then not take my taxes the next, then the following year take my tax returns again. Then they stopped taking my tax returns in recent years. And I've heard nothing from them at all.

Why? I have no clue.

To this day I am still unsure of the exact cause of the overpayment or even if there is one to begin with.

I feel have been fortunate thus far to have only been grazed by the random lightning bolts thrown by social security.

How long will my luck last? Could be till I retire. Could be over tomorrow. With social security, who knows? Thanks for taking the time to read this story/rant.

You might think that's a unique story. I did, until we started receiving more emails like this one. It appears Social Security's long hand reaches beyond the grave, and into the pockets of recipients who were children and never saw the money (except if their parents or guardians spent it on school clothes and books and food).

Jacob asks why, if a dependent child cannot actually receive benefits and they must be given to a guardian, the child should be held responsible for returning those benefits that Social Security claims were sent by mistake. Kyle faces a similar situation:

Hey, my name is Kyle. I live in Washington state. My mother died when I was 5 and my guardians received survivors benefits. I am now 31 years old around 2020 I got a letter saying I owed $11,000 for benefits my guardians got when I was a child and my mother passed away.

I filed several appeals and never got approved they literally told me they can do whatever they want so as of 2023 I have the balance paid in full due to wage garnishments and taking my tax returns.

I have actually overpaid them and they still are to write me a check for it and it's been paid in full for 6 months now. I thought I was the only one who this happened to. I still currently have all the documents of the case in filing but as of now it's paid in full and I'm down $11,000 of my money. Just thought I'd let you know.

Not all Social Security problems for young people start out with benefits received by their parents. Here's one more email, from Vickie, that illustrates the breadth and idiocy of Social Security clawbacks from those just starting out in the workforce.

In 1996 or '97, I can't remember the exact date, while attending college as a legally blind student, I received a letter from SSA informing me that I was overpaid by $900+. I didn't know what else to do but pay the amount back over 9 months. At about the same time, a fellow student with a different type of disability met a similar fate but for over $4,000.00. My friend said he wasn't going to pay it back. My husband received an overpayment letter from the SSA for over $4,000.00 in 2006. They called every single day until he could bring in a check.

These young adults are being clawed back by Social Security before they have barely started to work!

But Wait, There's More!

Just as we were going to press, another email came in with a story that transcends generations. And it also transcends logic, belief, and reality.
Audrey wrote:

In April of 2021, I received a letter from the Social Security Administration stating that I had received student benefits on my father's account and, when these benefits were terminated, an overpayment of $157.20 remained on the account. Further it stated, "The overpayment was for a month of nonattendance in high school."

In 2021 when I received this letter, I was 67 years old. I graduated from high school in 1971. I admit—I did skip a few English classes in the last semester of high school—but I do not believe I skipped an entire month of school! I received my high school diploma, as well as bachelor's and master's degrees. In addition, I do not think I received Social Security benefits in high school because my father was living and employed.

I did receive some Social Security benefits during graduate school, because my father had died and benefits could be paid (at that time) to full time students until age 23. However, the letter stated, inaccurately, it was during high school so I wonder if the overpayment was also inaccurate.

When I called the Social Security Administration, to discuss this, the first phone appointment available (this was during the time in person appointments were not available due to COVID) was on July 29. However, when I spoke to the representative on that date, I was told that the appointment was "too late" since the "overpayment" amount had already been deducted from my Social Security check received earlier in the month and my only choice was to appeal the decision. At that point, I decided this was not worth the time and effort for $157.20 so I did not submit an appeal.

*However, it is concerning to me that this clawback process
is occurring, apparently with inaccurate information, and
after such a delay—in my case, at least forty-four years.
The amount was minimal for me, but it could be much
more substantial for others—and other individuals may be
dependent on every dollar of their current benefit. I agree with
you—if the overpayment is due to a mistake by the Social
Security Administration, they need to take responsibility
for this and not clawback the money. There should be a
discontinuation of this arbitrary seemingly clawback
process or at least a statute of limitations.*

Social Security can't get its act together to straighten out benefits currently being paid. Yet it can reach back into the past—more than 40 years into the past—when today's adults were only children, to figure out a way to get them to make payments—or face losing their future Social Security benefits.

CHAPTER 7

A Final Clawback Horror Story

By now, you're surely outraged by these unbelievably cruel and sad stories. We've read them all, and frankly it was hard to choose among the most outrageous. We know you share our sadness and disgust that our nation's citizens are subject to this kind of treatment.

These stories are in full public view because Social Security reached out to beneficiaries to disclose their own mistakes. And because we have put the pieces of this puzzle together. But what about the ones we will never find? We're talking about the hidden errors, where Social Security misleads its claimants into taking a lifetime of lower benefits.

In the next section of our book, we move on to some of Larry's more sophisticated criticisms of the Social Security system and the outright frauds it has knowingly perpetrated on recipients. But first, here's a final clawback horror story from Lynne to turn your stomach.

On 12/22 on my SS personal page said that I had an overpayment over $4100. After your review (2/23) that was removed from my page. On 11/29/20, I received a letter stating that my Part B would be $144.60 and Part D would be $31.50. On 12/2/20, I received a letter stating that I owed $1735.30 for Part B and $706.80 . . . for Part D. I sent in that payment.

The letter also stated that my monthly premium for Medicare Part B is $289.20 beginning 1/20 and $297 beginning 1/21. I have no idea where these figures came from.

On 3/21/22 I received a letter stating that my monthly benefit was changed to $174.60 and the prior amount was incorrect. It said "my new monthly benefit on the other record will be $2,002.90. When the two benefits are together, the total amount does not change. I have no idea where any of these numbers came from.

A letter dated 11/24/21 stated that no payment is due at this time because of adjustments made to my benefits. When I contacted SS after receiving this letter, I was told that I have a credit of over $3200 and it's much easier for SS to use that as a credit than to reimburse me.

I then received a letter dated 11/29/21 stating that my benefit for Part B IRMAA is $59.40 for 2021. My Part D is $12.30.

I then received a letter dated the same 11/29/21 that my part B IRMAA is $57.80 and Part D is $12.20.

A third letter dated the same 11/29/21 stated that I owe SS $775.20 which I sent in to you in 3 installments ($258.40 each)

Another bill came to me stating that I owe $12.40 that was due in full by 1/25/22. That was also sent to you.

A letter dated 11/28/22 came to me stating that my monthly benefit was $163.80 as of 11/21. It then said my monthly benefit had increased to $173,50 beginning 12/21, It then said the payment was incorrect and should have been $174.60. . . . as of 1/22. The same letter stated that my monthly benefit is $189.70 beginning 12/22 because of COLA.

Finally, it said that you are withholding all of my monthly payments beginning 12/22 to recover an overpayment and past due medical insurance payments. That same letter indicated that I will receive $67.10 for 6/23 around 7/23.

I sent in another 238.10 in December to make sure that my Medicare would be covered.

I know what I have paid you, but I cannot figure out why I would owe you $3,445.60.

After receiving all of this conflicting correspondence, and only verbally hearing that I don't owe anything is concerning. My current benefit should more than cover my Medicare payments. Even if my benefit did not cover all of my Medicare, it should have covered most of it.

When I told Ms. Biegansk that none of this made sense to me, she told me she totally understands, but this is out of her hands. She doesn't handle this part of SS.

She gave me all the information that she possibly could, but this needs to go to the other department which deals with the breakdowns of payments and benefits. I have waited too long to now hear that I have to put in an appeal and wait a long time to hear back from you. This is unacceptable and I would like this resolved as soon as possible before I receive another letter stating that I owe you MORE money! I need to get something in writing from you and according to my figures . . . SS owes me money toward my benefit.

So there you have it—unedited and authentic. Social Security cannot hide behind percentages and statistics when it is destroying the lives of real people and not only ignoring the plight of its recipients but adding to their personal financial disasters.

PART 2

Social Security Scams

CHAPTER 8

Social Security's Foundational Scam

Nobody would believe the Social Security horror stories we've just related—direct from the victims. They describe a system that's mean-spirited, heartless, cruel, and, well, choose your own words. They also depict government dysfunction that defies belief.

This is a system that is replete with indecipherable rules about indecipherable rules about indecipherable rules. It is run by an ancient computer system that no one can control. It's known for mailing random, bizarre benefit statements and churning out clawback demand letters on autopilot. It is defined by bureaucratic runarounds that set world records for delays, by administrators pretending their hands are tied, and by soulless politicians looking the other way.

The Social Security system claws back 80-year-olds for 45-year-old overpayments it doesn't bother proving; hits up 25-year-olds for supposedly mistaken benefits "received" at age 2; sues 5-year-olds weeks after their mother has been killed in a car accident; kicks people off disability for accidentally earning a few extra bucks; denies appeals based on indigency because the impoverished, disabled victim's cable plan has too many channels ("proving she's rich"); automatically terminates benefits of clawback victims despite those victims having no other means of support.

This unabashed financial abuse is grounded in Social Security's inhumane standard operating procedure. The overriding attitude of the Social Security administration has become its motto: "Our mistake is your problem!"

Would such a system . . .

- Run a massive Ponzi scheme, but try to disguise the fact as well as the magnitude of its insolvency?

- Scam over 10,000 widow(er)s out of more than $130 million?

- Falsely convince millions of early retirees that returning to work will cost them years of benefits?

- Bribe people in their late sixties to take benefits early without explaining the long-term cost?

- Provide some workers not a penny in extra benefits in exchange for years of FICA contributions?

- Tell survivors that their widow(er) and divorced widow(er) benefits peak at full retirement age when they may peak years earlier—costing survivors tens of thousands of dollars?

- Repeatedly emphasize life expectancy on its website and in its communications, thereby encouraging workers to take their benefits far too early at a generally huge lifetime benefit loss?

The answer is yes. Social Security does all these things.

Which of these behaviors are intentional? Which are commission by omission (leaving out relevant information)? Which are malevolence by staffers, and which are straight-out mistakes? We can't say, for sure. But the answer doesn't matter for you. Your goals are simple—understand the traps, avoid them, and warn others.

Before getting into the weeds, let me address a question you are surely asking. Why would Social Security scam widow(er)s or try to keep retirees from returning to work or do all the other awful things described in this chapter? Is it to save Social Security money? Is it to purposely create financial harm? Or is it just following the rules—the orders issued by Congress?

We think it's mostly the lack of leadership at the top— by Social Security's commissioners or acting commissioners, by members of Congress, by its trustees, and by the occupant of the Oval Office. Harry Truman famously said, "the buck stops here." With Social Security, "the buck stops there." Hopefully, this book will light a fire under everyone in government, from the president on down, to produce a Social Security system of which we can be proud rather than afraid.

How can a generally well-intentioned government agency be so duplicitous? It's ingrained from birth. The system's original, biggest, and most dangerous lie involves its financing.

Social Security Is and Always Has Been a Ponzi Scheme

Social Security's funding—actually, lack of funding—is the "original sin" when it comes to lies and deception. Social Security has been running a Ponzi scheme since its founding 88 years ago. In choosing this method of finance, but pretending otherwise by describing the system as pay-go, opacity, duplicity, and deception became, from the get-go, accepted practice—part of Social Security's DNA to be utilized as needed.

Check the meaning of pay-as-you-go at investopedia.com. It suggests a saving system, similar to an IRA or 401(k) system, to which workers contribute, with some flexibility and some ability to direct investments. This bears essentially no connection to how Social Security works.

Yet, at Social Security's website, www.ssa.gov, we're told Social Security is financed by a payroll tax, half of which is paid by our employers. Then we're told contributions are made to the system's interest-earning Trust Fund, suggesting that what we eventually receive from the system will reflect what we put plus an investment return determined by the Fund.

This brief description is about as distant from the truth as it gets. There is no use of the term "Ponzi scheme," no confession that one's contributions aren't, to any real degree, invested. There is no admission that the Trust Fund is a flow-through entity which, almost exclusively, takes contributions from young people and hands them to old people. It never explains clearly that our benefits are set by a formula, not repayment of contributions plus investment returns, and that payment to retirees of promised benefits (enshrined by formula) is conditional on the system receiving enough contributions from current workers.

When Pay As You Go Means Pray As You Go

The real meaning of pay-as-you-go is this: *You go and pay to others and then pray that others, many not yet born, will pay to you.* Even the National Academy of Social Insurance, Social Security's primary water boy, gets this right. But nowhere does the Academy describe the system as a Ponzi scheme whose intricate benefit calculations will go poof if demographics, labor force participation, inequality in wages, and labor productivity growth all undermine what's paid in and, thus, what can be paid out.

In contrast to Social Security's abbreviated balderdash, full disclosure of the system's financing in total honesty would sound more like this:

> Remember Charles Ponzi? Well, we're setting up the same "sure-thing" saving and investment system for you. So hand over your FICA contributions and let us gamble with your future and that of your children. If there aren't enough of them or they aren't sufficiently productive, we'll need to give you less of their money or take more from your kids.
>
> We call your payroll taxes contributions in order to make participating in Social Security sound like you're enrolled in a fully funded saving system. And, to enhance that hoax, we're recording your earnings histories and specifying an exact benefit formula that ties your future benefits to your past and projected contributions. We're even going to provide statements with your projected benefits.
>
> And, to make you think you're getting a truly fabulous return on your investment, we're going to claim that half of your FICA contributions aren't made by you, but by your magnanimous employer. Do we realize that employers will reduce your pay

dollar for dollar based on what they are forced to pay on your behalf? Of course. We're not stupid. But we're counting on you to be stupid—to the point of forgetting what we just told you.

But if you do manage to recognize our word game, don't tell anyone. You'll spoil our marvelous deception. Imagine persuading the entire workforce that they're paying only half of their actual taxes. That's a feat that even Charley couldn't pull off.

Oh, and by the way, we're going to set up a Social Security Trust Fund to further suggest we're investing contributions we receive, rather than handing them directly to millions of outstretched hands the minute they come in the door. So, yes, the Trust Fund will be miniscule.

But we don't expect anyone to notice. And if you're one of those that does, please keep it quiet.

Social Security's Original Sins—
Pretense and Deceit

Failure to make this disclosure in plain English at the system's inception is Social Security's original and ongoing sin. As any fifth grader can explain, chain letters rob Peter to pay Paul and then rob Matthew to pay Peter, and on it goes. If not enough new, well-paid participants show up or too many beneficiaries refuse to die on time (at their life expectancies)—all situations our country now faces—the "security" in Social Security goes out the window. Stated differently, all the intricate mathematical formulas that specify to the penny what you'll get back based on what you put in can go poof the instant the system can't force enough workers to pay what's needed to meet its promises—promises that were, from day one, grounded in hope and prayer.

All this said, Social Security has had a good run. It's nearing its granite (90th) birthday and hasn't missed a payment. Why then all this talk about duplicitous funding? Things aren't falling apart.

Actually, they are, and at a rapid clip. Our country is aging, and the covered wage base from which Social Security takes as it goes isn't keeping up. The reasons are clear—too few young people collectively earning too little to pay the massive baby boom generation. The baby boomers have just retired. Listen carefully and you'll hear them chanting two words, which they will repeat until their dying day: "Pay Me!"

Social Security's Worst Horror Story— It's Beyond Broke

Ponzi schemes are built to fail. As any fifth grader will explain it, once the chain letter has been sold to everyone in the class, there's no one left to buy it. Social Security's Ponzi scheme is in the process of failing—*spectacularly*. Its unfunded liability—the present value difference between projected outlays and receipts less the Trust Fund—is a colossal $65.9 trillion. You can find this figure in Table VI.F1 of Social Security's March 31, 2023 Trustees Report. It was calculated by Social Security's fabled Office of the Actuaries, who are consummate professionals.

Wrapping one's brain around $65.9 trillion isn't easy. It's miles larger than our nation's official debt. And almost exactly 2.5 years of GDP. Everyone in the country would need to work for two and a half years, consume absolutely nothing, paying every penny they earned into Social Security's Trust Fund to give it the wherewithal to meet all future formulaic benefit obligations.

As with the official debt, our politicians' clear intent is to dump this astronomical bill in our children's laps. Their method? Most likely it will include phased-in increases in the system's full retirement age, gradually phased-in benefit cuts targeted toward those with higher incomes, FICA tax hikes, also targeted to high earners, increased federal income taxation of benefits, and other policy moves. The phase-ins will be long enough to leave most of the elderly and near elderly mostly off the hook. When will this "fix" happen? Like the 1983 Greenspan Commission, our leaders will wait until the Trust Fund is a couple of months from running completely dry—and then form a bipartisan commission to enact a grand reform.

The Third Rail Is Deadly for a Reason—
Retirees Have Plenty of Free Time to Vote

Why will the reforms end up so generationally unfair? Because children and future generations don't vote and young and middle-aged adults are working on election day. The elderly, on the other hand, vote in droves. This is why politicians call Social Security the third rail. You touch it, as in reducing current retirees' benefits, and your political career is toast.

As with the Greenspan Commission, the next commission will be packed with politicians who care far more about the next election than the next generation. Consequently, they, too, will do too little too late. This is why Social Security's long-term insolvency is almost twice as bad today as it was in 1982. Then the system needed a 20 percent immediate and permanent percentage point hike in the FICA tax to cover all future benefit obligations. Today, the system needs a 37 percent hike; i.e., the current 12.4 percent FICA tax needs to be set forever at 17 percent. Delay is no option for our children. It leaves more of today's adults off the hook, thereby raising the tax hike their children will face. Seventeen percent is far higher than the roughly 13 percent sustainable payroll tax rate calculated in 1983.

Too Little Is Too Late

A good analogy for this reliable, kick-the-can process is a patient with a malignant but operable tumor. Rather than remove the entire tumor, the surgeon takes out, say, 35 percent and says, "Come see me in a year." A year later, the tumor's significantly larger than before the surgery. Again, the surgeon removes 35 percent and leaves the rest for the following year. This provides the surgeon a steady flow of income for a while. After a few years of surgeries, the patient misses her appointment—for good reason. She's dead.

Pretending to Do Long-Term Planning

In Social Security's case, the politicians have established a convenient, if economically vacuous, mathematic measure for doing too little too late. Rather than consider Social Security's unfunded liability over the entire future horizon, they truncate their analysis of the system's finances at exactly 75 years. Not 75.7 years or 51.1 years, but 75.0 years. Why this duration?

In donning 75-year blinders, the politicians reduce the system's unfunded liability by two-thirds! Their mantra is, "The future is uncertain. Seventy-five years is far enough ahead to look." The technical description of this judgment is first-order stupid. Most of today's newborns will be retired and collecting their benefits in 75 years. Truncating your projections at 75 years effectively assumes they and everyone else alive in 2097 will simultaneously drop dead on January 1, 2098. No one in Congress buys that assumption. Its adoption of the 75-year time horizon is simply part of disguising Social Security's Ponzi scheme at future generations' expense.

Moreover, as an economist I'm compelled to point out that when things are uncertain, policymakers have a fiduciary obligation to focus on worst-case scenarios. In Social Security's case, the 75-year horizon is, arguably, predicated on the notion that the growing cash flow deficits that the actuaries project in years 76 and beyond will miraculously disappear. Good luck with that.

Hiding the Bacon

Even the 75-year unfunded liability is kept under wraps to the extent possible. Google "federal debt" and you'll come up with a vast number of hits. Next Google "Social Security's unfunded liability." Hardly anything comes up. That's no accident. In addition to successfully disguising its Ponzi scheme for close to a century, Social Security has been marvelously adept at hiding how badly it's failing. Look up Table VI.F1 in the system's Trustees Report. The table is stuck deep in the Appendix, where no one will see it. Once you find the table, you'll see the infinite horizon (untruncated liability) of $65.9 trillion. You'll also see the 75-year red ink. It's $22.4 trillion.

When the 2023 Trustees Report appeared with its $65.9 trillion reported unfunded infinite horizon liability—some $10 trillion larger than it had been just a few years earlier—I searched the web for articles about this enormous obligation. Nothing. In years past, it was the same story. If the press mentioned anything about Social Security's red ink, it was about the 75-year unfunded liability.

Ok, I've now done what I promised Terry not to do—playing economist and telling you about the system's macro financial condition. But the point was not about that terrible dilemma. The point was to clarify that lying, dissembling, and scamming—indeed, running a Ponzi scheme so massive that Charles and Bernie would blush—come quite naturally to Social Security. Given this, should we expect to find scams and deceptions permeating the system's substructure? Unfortunately, yes.

CHAPTER 9

The Use-It-or-Lose-It-Scam

ocial Security provides 12 different benefits (see box on page 86). All workers who have paid into the system for 10 or more years are eligible to receive their retirement benefit. The other benefits are called dependent benefits because they are paid to current or former relatives of the worker under a highly complex set of conditions. Most workers paying FICA taxes know about the system's retirement benefits. But many, perhaps most Americans are entirely unaware of the 11 dependent benefits for which they are or may become eligible.

Social Security makes no effort to directly inform any of us about our eligibility for any of its benefits. Both Terry and I have answered a sad question from workers in their mid-seventies. "I'm still working. Can I collect my retirement benefit?"

Of course, they can. There is no earnings test after reaching full retirement, not to mention, as described below, that the earnings test is its own scam. And, after age 70, Social Security provides no delayed retirement credits, which compensate you for waiting to collect. Those credits are provided to take into account that every month you wait to collect beyond full retirement age you are taking a chance of dying and, thus, missing out on your retirement benefits. A similar compensation for delaying benefit receipt occurs before full retirement age. It's called the early retirement reduction. The compensation for waiting is simply not having your benefit reduced.

A person checking in at 75 years old will have lost 4.5 years of benefits by not filing for his or her retirement benefit at 70. Why 4.5?

Because Social Security will only pay foregone benefits six months in arrears.

Does Social Security make any attempt to contact you if it knows a month of retirement benefits is being lost for good every month you don't file for the benefit? None whatsoever. Could it? Certainly. It has your latest address on file. Social Security doesn't currently have our phone numbers or email addresses, but it could easily solicit them and use them to send general messages. Here's an example:

"If you've reached age 70, there is no incentive to wait to collect your retirement benefit. Please call us today to file."

Social Security could also start sending your benefit automatically when you reach age 70. After all, it's your money. Withholding it without making a good faith effort to transmit it is both shameful and a scam. At a minimum, the system should be running radio, internet, newspaper, and other media ads asking a simple question. "Are you aware of all your available Social Security benefits and have you planned your optimal collection strategy? If not, call us at this number, check out this website, or email us at this address."

Losing Over $1.5 Million in Divorced Widow's Benefits Through Lack of Notification and Knowledge

Larry and his wife recently took their 96-year-old friend, Debbie, to dinner. Debbie is a working therapist who does yoga daily. And because she's working, she's paying FICA. Hence, Social Security knows her address and her bank account information. It wires Debbie's measly retirement benefit to her account each month.

Debbie had three husbands. The first, Sam, she divorced after roughly 20 years. He was a very high earner. The other two, not so much.

Larry: Are you collecting divorced widow's benefits based on Sam's work record?

Debbie: Sam's long gone.

Larry: You can still collect. Actually, you could have been collecting for the last 36 years.

Debbie: What do you mean?

Larry: I'm talking about divorcée survivor benefits. You'll need to prove you were married for 10-plus years and then got divorced. Do you have your marriage certificate and divorce decree?

Debbie: Are you nuts? I was 16 when I married and 36 when I divorced. You think I still have those records?

Larry: Do you know where you were married and where you filed for divorce?

Debbie: This I know.

Larry: Great. We'll go online, order the records, and help you file. My guess is you'll start collecting about $3,500 per month. Unfortunately, Social Security's failure to notify you has cost you over $1.5 million dollars, cumulated through today.

Debbie: Why didn't they tell me?" They knew we were married and that Sam had died. They also had my address.

Larry: You will soon have a far higher income, but you have lost decades of income—over $1 million if cumulated to the present.

Not directly informing people who haven't collected benefits for which they are eligible is malfeasance, plain and simple.

Social Security's Myriad Provisions

Whether or not you've heard of all 12 of the system's benefits, you surely haven't heard of all of the major elements determining the check you or your parents or your kids or your uncle receive every month. It's the very same check (or electronic deposit) that may be clawed back in tomorrow's mail.

Social Security's 12 Benefits

1. Retirement Benefits	7. Widow(er) Benefits
2. Spousal Benefits	8. Divorced Widow(er) Benefits
3. Divorced Spousal Benefits	9. Mother and Father Benefits
4. Children Benefits	10. Parent Benefits
5. Disabled Child Benefits	11. Disability Benefits
6. Child-in-Care Spousal Benefits	12. Death Benefits

These provisions, which are immensely complex on their own, let alone in concert, aren't innocent when it comes to the use-it-or-lose-it scam. If people get these provisions wrong, they may incorrectly think they aren't eligible for particular benefits. And, as we know, if they aren't requested, they are lost.

An example is the government pension offset provision, which reduces dependent benefits received by workers receiving a pension from noncovered employment. If the pension is two-thirds or more the size of the dependent benefit, it's wiped out.

Hypothetical Sally might check with Social Security at, say, age 65 and learn that she's not able to collect a penny in widow's benefits on her deceased spouse's work record. Now fast forward 20 years and assume prices have risen by a factor of 40 percent. If Sally's pension is not inflation adjusted, she may well have become eligible to collect a widow's benefit. That's because her widow's benefit will have risen by 40 percent thanks to Social Security's annual cost-of-living (COLA) inflation adjustment. And two-thirds of the original pension may now fall far short of Sally's widow's benefit. Hence, she'll be able to collect the difference.

Social Security will, of course, not bother to inform Sally that she's leaving benefits on the table. As for Sally, she'll, probably have no clue this is happening. Why would she? The staffers at Social Security likely weren't trained to inform the Sallys they "help" to check every year to see if they have become eligible to collect.

Social Security's Major Benefit Provisions

1. Calculation of Quarters of Coverage
2. Determining Computation Years
3. Wage Indexing
4. Average Indexed Monthly Earnings
5. PIA Formula
6. Early Benefit Reduction Factors
7. Deeming
8. Delayed Retirement Credit
9. The Earnings Test
10. The Windfall Elimination Provision (WEP)
11. The Government Pension Offset Provision (GPO)
12. The Adjustment of the Reduction Factor
13. The COLA Benefit Adjustment
14. The RIBLIM Widow(er)'s Benefit Formula
15. The Family Benefit Maximum
16. The Joint Family Benefit Maximum
17. Disabled Worker Family Benefit Maximum
18. The Recomputation of Benefits
19. The Incomplete Inflation Indexation of the Benefit Formula
20. The Windex Formula

Do Social Security's Benefit Calculators Help?

Social Security provides a simplistic calculator as well as more detailed online calculators that you can access at SSA.gov. The simplistic calculator is not good enough for government work. To use the more detailed calculators you'll have to create a My Social Security secure account. This computation will access your own earnings record and allow you to compute any offsets such as the WEP, which can reduce your individual benefit payments.

This sounds straightforward until you realize that establishing your online SSA account is no minor task. You can spend hours or days trying to establish your identity with Social Security only to be kicked off its system with no explanation. You'll then wait hours on the phone to connect with a Social Security rep who has nothing to say except "try again in a couple of days." It took Larry three attempts over two weeks to set up his account. As for Terry, she, like so many others, has given up.

Even if you make it into Social Security's system, its calculators don't include the earnings records of your spouse, dead or alive, let alone your ex-spouses, let alone your dead exes. Nor do they include key information like whether your dead spouse or dead ex took retirement benefits early, or when your current spouse started taking retirement benefits.

All this information is important for calculating your best claiming strategy since your best strategy depends on your spouse's earnings history and vice versa. Equally distressing—the SSA benefit calculators adopt, as discussed below, bizarre assumptions about the economy. These include no future inflation and no future economy-wide growth in wages. Yet, your claiming decision is designed to cover your lifetime of expected benefits, and it is irrevocable.

In short, Social Security's calculators do not really help us navigate its ridiculously complex benefit-claiming provisions with their myriad catch 22s. Does it make sense to claim on your deceased spouse's record first, then switch to your own? What's the real impact of claiming early, but continuing to earn income from work? How much more do you get in lifetime benefits from collecting at 70 versus, say, 63? How does a government pension reduce your earned Social Security benefit from work in covered employment? How much does additional work in the covered sector raise your years of substantial earnings and, thereby, lower the WEP?

How can you get correct answers to these significant questions? In addition to writing a best-selling book demystifying Social Security, Larry has created two online tools—MaxiFi Planner (maxifi.com) and Maximize My Social Security (maximizemysocialsecurity.com).

MaxiFi Planner does full lifetime financial planning, including Social Security lifetime benefit maximization. Maximize My Social Security shares the same Social Security code with MaxiFi but focuses simply on ensuring you receive your highest lifetime benefits. Both tools are very inexpensive, but incredibly powerful. They consider all available family benefit collection strategies, which can number in the tens of thousands, and determine precisely which one yields the highest lifetime payout.

But as we continue to reveal these horror stories, we have another consideration in mind. Is the complexity of Social Security just an ordinary bureaucratic nightmare that has grown like kudzu over the years? Or could something more nefarious be at work here?

Consider the possibility that these byzantine rules are designed to help cover up the system's foundational flaw. Having a zillion rules about your particular benefits certainly averts one's mind from the possibility that none of those rules will matter because the system will go broke before you are able to collect.

CHAPTER 10

The Widows Scam

started exposing the widows scam almost a decade ago thanks to a whistle-blower named John Adams. John worked (still does) at one of Social Security's offices in Philadelphia. His job is serving as a technical expert. When he discovered the widows scam, John started writing letters up the food chain. He also contacted me. I then started writing columns about the scam on the *PBS NewsHour* website, in *Forbes*, in my Substack, in my co-authored book, *Get What's Yours: The Secrets to Maxing Out Your Social Security*, and in my latest book, *Money Magic*.

My tag-team effort with John seemed to pay off in 2018. That's when Social Security's Inspector General's office, sufficiently embarrassed by three years of negative publicity, moved its torpid self to investigate. What did it find? Something quite horrific. The IG identified over 13,000 widow(er)s who had been conned out of over $130 million in benefits! And, as the IG made clear, this big con was ongoing, with more people falling prey every day. The IG also told Social Security to end the scam immediately and identify and reimburse its victim.

Today, five years after the IG report, nothing's been done. The scam is ongoing. Worse still, the Inspector General's report is no longer publicly available. The link to the report, which was https://oig.ssa.gov/sites/default/files/audit/full/pdf/A-09-18-50559.pdf, now comes back with "Page not found." It should come back with "Our mistake is your problem."

I'll explain the diabolically simple workings of the widows scam momentarily. It involves a mistake in software coding that Social Security could easily have fixed and can do so today. Then I'll explain Social Security's retirement trap scam as well as other scams, loopholes, and catch 22s. The goal is not to further depress, deflate, or demoralize you. The goal is to keep you safe from Social Security's clutches. Those are strong words coming from someone who fully appreciates the enormous good Social Security does and is trying to do. But the good doesn't excuse the bad, let alone the awful and horrific.

How the Widows Scam Works

How does the widows scam work? Before explaining, let me be clear. No one in Social Security has to my or Terry's knowledge ever explicitly instructed the staff to scam a widow(er) or anyone else. Yet, in not taking steps to stop entrapping widows, Social Security is perpetuating what can only be described as a scam.

Clearly, senior-level people in the Social Security Administration know about the widows scam. They also know their 60K-plus staff has not been formally trained to prevent its occurrence, that no one has fixed their computer system to ensure that the practice does not continue, and that they have failed to identify scammed widow(er)s and compensate them or their heirs.

Fraud is defined in the dictionary as "wrongful deception intended to result in financial gain." I think not telling widow(er)s what they need to know and, thereby, intentionally or not, saving the system money fits that definition.

The widow(er)s scam entails forcing, cajoling, persuading, conning, manipulating, or simply allowing unknowing widow(er)s under 70 to file simultaneously for both their widow(er)s and their retirement benefits. Doing so prevents widow(er)s from taking one benefit first and the other later, after it has grown—*potentially enormously.*

Once you file for a Social Security benefit, it can no longer grow even if you aren't effectively receiving it. And the only exception to this rule is if you've withdrawn your benefit or, in the case of your retirement benefit, you've suspended it.

Let me illustrate the scam using my software company's Maximize My Social Security program. I'll take the case of a hypothetical retired widow named Sue who just turned 62. Her hypothetical husband, Bill, recently died.

Sue has some immediate options. She can file for her widow's benefit, she can file for her retirement benefit, or she can file for both. If she files for both, she won't collect both. Instead, she'll collect the larger of the two.

But filing for a benefit—as in checking a filing box on a Social Security form or having someone, potentially without your knowledge, check the box, either by using a pen on a printed form or electronically on a keyboard—has major ramifications. It means you technically start receiving that benefit immediately, *even if you don't receive it!* And it means you can't file and start that benefit at a later date when it is potentially far larger.

I want this to be completely clear: Checking the file-me-for-benefit-X box tells Social Security you've opted to begin benefit X right away *even if you don't receive a penny of that benefit because it's lower than another benefit you've also opted to start receiving.*

If filing for benefit X produces no additional benefits, benefit X is a phantom benefit—one you don't receive—but is treated as being received for the purpose of determining whether you have delayed taking the benefit.

An example will help. Here's how Sue got scammed:

Sue's Retirement Benefit. If Sue files for her retirement benefit, whether voluntarily or involuntarily, at 62, it will be $26,199 per year. If she files at 70 for her retirement benefit, it will equal $46,131 (measured in today's dollars) per year. That's a whopping 76 percent higher!

Why the 76 percent increase? Two reasons. First, Sue's benefit is substantially reduced because she filed before her full retirement age. Second, by waiting to file *beyond* full retirement age, which is 67 in

Sue's case, she accrues delayed retirement credits for each month she waits to file through age 70.

Sue's Widow's Benefit. If Sue voluntarily or involuntarily files for her widow's benefit at 62, it will, according to the example I developed, be $27,200 per year—just $1 larger than her age 62 retirement benefit.

Delayed Retirement Benefits

Every month beyond our full retirement age (FRA) and the month we turn 70 that we delay filing for our retirement benefit, the benefit amount increases by 8/12 percent. If Sue delays filing for her retirement benefit till 70, which is 24 months after reaching full retirement, her retirement benefit starting at 70 is 24 percent (36 months times 8/12 percent) higher than if she files for it starting at 67. And to repeat, it's 76 percent higher than if she files for her benefit upon turning 62.

But if she files for her widow's benefit later, it won't be reduced or will be reduced by less. Delayed retirement credits apply only to retirement benefits. Hence, waiting beyond FRA to file for your widow's benefit never pays. But unless a widow is in dire financial straits, she (or he) should never file for a widow(er)'s benefit before full retirement age!

But, as you'll soon see, the widow's benefit may stop growing long before FRA.

Sue Files or Is Filed for Both Benefits at Age 62. If Sue files before her FRA, she will receive the larger of the two reduced benefits, namely her $27,200 widow's benefit. In filing (or being filed for) her own retirement benefit at 62, she has effectively stopped its growth dead in the tracks.

And, since $27,200 exceeds Sue's own $27,199 benefit, Sue will be deemed to collect her widow's benefit—and *only* her widow's benefit—for the rest of her life. And she will never receive a penny of her retirement benefit for which she contributed her entire working life! She will receive only her widow's benefit, which is substantially and permanently reduced because she claimed her widow's benefit before her own full retirement age.

In short, by physically or electronically checking a box or having a box checked for her by an untrained or malevolent Social Security staffer, Sue's own retirement benefit is gone forever.

Sue Files Just for Her Widow's Benefit at Age 62 and Waits Until Age 70 to File for Her Retirement Benefit. In this case, Sue receives her $27,200 widow's benefit from 62 through 70 and a $46,131 retirement benefit from age 70 on. To initiate this strategy, she would check only the widow's benefit, <u>not</u> her own retirement benefit, when she applies.

Sue Visits Her Local Social Security Office. Let's consider how easily Sue can become a victim of this Social Security horror story. Assume that Sue visits her local Social Security office at age 62. There she meets Mabel, a well-meaning staffer who is knows just enough to be dangerous.

Let's listen to Mabel.

> "Sue, you're 62. You're getting on in age. You should file now for every benefit you can. Otherwise, you'll miss out if you die young."

This is first-order stupid. If Sue dies young, she'll be in heaven and won't be kicking herself over lost benefits. In heaven you can have as much money as your heart desires in whatever currency you'd like.

Sue looks at Mabel's sweet, knowing face and says, "Of course. Sign me up for all the benefits available." What Sue doesn't realize and what Mabel doesn't get is that Sue can't receive both her retirement and widow's benefits, just the larger of the two.

The Con Within the Con

In Mabel's defense, Social Security tells its staff that widow(er)s who file for both benefits at the same time always receive their retirement benefit plus their widow's benefit, but not the standard widow's benefit. Rather it's the *excess widow(er)'s benefit*. The excess widow's benefit is defined as the full widow's benefit less the retirement benefit (zero if the difference is negative). The retirement benefit plus the excess widow's benefit equals the full widow's benefit. Hence, although Social Security could teach Mabel that Sue will get the larger of the two benefits, it trains her that Sue will collect two benefits. This is the basis of Social Security's conning millions of workers into thinking their payroll tax contributions deliver higher benefits when nothing could be further from the truth.

Sue's Humongous Loss in Lifetime Benefits. Mabel dually files Sue for both her widow's and retirement benefit. By checking a box, in this case the retirement-benefit application box, Sue instantly loses $436,821 in lifetime benefits. That's roughly 10 years of her pre-retirement, after-tax earnings. By following the advice of her Social Security contact, Sue has been scammed out of nearly half a million dollars!

Present Values

The $436,821 is a present value. It takes account of the fact that money received in the future isn't as valuable as money received today. This makes common sense. A given amount of money, call it X, in your hands today can be invested, producing more than X in future years.

Sue's Trip to Social Security at Age 70. Fast forward a few years. Sue is a month away from reaching 70 and has a conversation with her friend, Marleen. Marleen is single and explains that she's waiting until age 70 to collect her retirement benefit. "It's going to be 76 percent larger starting at 70 than had I started it when I retired at 62," she says.

Sue tells Marleen, "I'm doing the same. Right now, I'm receiving just my widow's benefit. Next month, when I turn 70, I'm going to have them send me my retirement benefit. It's going to be 76 percent larger than what I'm now collecting. Knowing I'm getting so much more starting at 70 has let me afford to travel. In fact, I've taken an expensive cruise in each of the past eight years—cruises I could never have afforded otherwise."

A month later, Sue heads back to her local Social Security office. Mabel is long gone—promoted to supervisor in another office across the country. Sue meets with Margo and says she wants to register for her retirement benefit.

Margo checks on her computer. "Sue, you already filed for your retirement benefit—eight years ago, at the same time you filed for your widow's benefit. You've been receiving your widows benefit ever since because it was the larger of the two."

Sue says, "Yes, I know. I haven't been receiving my retirement benefit. I want to start collecting it beginning next month at its 76 percent higher value because I waited until I'm 70."

Margo says, "Sorry Sue, but since you filed for your retirement benefit eight years ago, the system treats you as having received it. You can't file for it from scratch again. You took it early, so you can't receive a higher benefit reserved for those who gave up receiving the benefit for eight years."

Sue, her blood pressure boiling, says, "I never received a penny of my retirement benefit. Check what you sent me. You only sent me my widow's benefit. I've waited eight long years to collect my retirement benefit. I need that money. I demand that money."

Margo smiles and says, "Sue. It's right here in the system. You filed for your retirement benefit at age 62. You've been receiving it for eight years. The reason it never hit your checking account is clear. Your widow's benefit was larger. I'm sorry, Sue, but I can't do anything. You chose to collect your retirement benefits early and can't pretend now to have done otherwise."

Sue becomes apoplectic. She screams. "I never filed for anything. A woman named Mabel set things up. She asked me if I wanted to collect both benefits. I said yes. But only one came. So, I realized she only signed me up for my widow's benefit. I demand to see a supervisor."

Margo smiles. "Sue, we're short-staffed. I am the supervisor. And regardless of what Mabel told you, you filed for your retirement benefit at 62 and have been getting it ever since. The fact that it was superseded by an even higher widow's benefit was a good thing. You received, as far as I can see, an extra dollar each year for the last eight years because the widow's benefit was a dollar higher.

"You can appeal, but I wouldn't recommend it. It can take years to get a hearing. You'll need to prove we made a mistake—for which you have no evidence. And, even if you had, you need to prove not only that we made a mistake, but that you are poor. The administrative judge who decides will look at all your past expenses. If you've done things like take a cruise, the judge will turn you down even if it was our mistake, which it clearly wasn't."

"There Must Be Some Way Out of Here Said the Joker to the Thief"—Bob Dylan

So now it's clear: If Sue files for her retirement benefit at 62, it will be reduced due to her "taking it" early even though she receives nothing from this phantom benefit. And it won't grow after she reaches full retirement age via the accrual of delayed retirement credits.

There were two ways Sue could have eliminated or at least limited her original mistake. If she had realized that her retirement benefit had been activated, she could have filed to withdraw it. Withdrawal applications for benefits are accepted if submitted within a year of the benefits initiation *provided all benefits received are repaid.*

In Sue's case, Social Security would claim that she received her retirement benefit plus an excess widow's benefit and force her to repay her retirement benefit for all months she received benefits even though she effectively never received a penny of her retirement benefit.

If Sue hadn't withdrawn her retirement benefit, she could have suspended it at FRA. That would have allowed her to collect delayed retirement credits until age 70, when she would restart her retirement benefit.

During the years when her retirement benefit was in suspension, she would have still been collecting her widow's benefit.

But for Sue to do either of these things she would have needed to know that she was officially receiving her retirement benefit—when she really wasn't. And clearly, Social Security wasn't about to volunteer this important information. So, at age 70, Sue has forfeited nearly half a million dollars in well-deserved Social Security benefits.

The Size of the Widows Scam

The Inspector General identified 13,514 widows and widowers who are owed over $130 million due to the widows scam. And these data are from 2018. Rather than end the scam and reimburse its victims, Social Security has ignored the IG and scammed thousands more. How can you avoid the widows scam? It's actually very easy as we'll explain in our conclusions.

CHAPTER 11

The Retirement Trap Scam

This scam costs millions of Americans years of lost labor income. It costs Uncle Sam a commensurate huge loss in tax revenue. It revolves around the "earnings test"—popularly known as a "penalty" for taking Social Security before full retirement age, while continuing to earn income from work.

Scams usually benefit the scammer. This one—Uncle Sam's conning early retirees not to earn beyond a pittance—entails the scammer shooting himself in the foot. It represents perhaps the worst policy our politicians have yet devised.

Social Security, as we've seen, dissembles, disguises, and deceives on a routine basis. The problem is congenital, habitual, and intentional. It's been lying from birth about the nature of its financing to obscure its underlying Ponzi scheme. It routinely scams widows to maintain the illusion that everyone who pays FICA payroll taxes receives retirement benefits. And it combines its ostensibly draconian—but fundamentally fake—"earnings test" to uphold an almost century-old founding principle: *If you are able-bodied, you need to work, not laze about and collect benefits.*

The earnings test reduces benefits paid to early beneficiaries (those collecting benefits before FRA) if they earn above certain thresholds. This tax on labor (wages and self-employment) income doesn't come out of a worker's paycheck. Instead, it is taken out of the benefits one would otherwise receive.

As of 2023, beneficiaries who don't reach FRA in the current calendar year will lose 50 cents on the dollar in benefits for every dollar earned above $21,240 in 2023. Beneficiaries who do reach FRA in the current calendar year lose 33 cents on the dollar in benefits for each dollar earned above $56,520 in 2022.

Taxing people's labor at these draconian rates when they already face substantial federal payroll, federal income, state income, and sales taxes is meant to do just one thing—get them to exit the workforce.

Social Security goes out of its way to explain the earnings test: *Take benefits early and live by our principle that those who can work shouldn't be allowed to collect.*

Yes, you can flip burgers at McDonald's. But earn beyond your relevant threshold and you will be taxed senseless. So, if you've opted to collect early, you can paint, bowl, fish, exercise, read books, play D&D, travel, meditate, play bridge, do whatever you want—except earn much money. If you do earn more than peanuts, Social Security will make sure you end up working for next to nothing.

The Big Lie Underlying the Retirement Trap Scam

Social Security intentionally portrays its earnings test as a confiscatory tax levied on early beneficiaries who earn beyond a very low threshold. In truth, it's nothing of the sort. Instead, the earnings test is a phony tax.

Here's why. Every dollar taxed away by the earnings test is returned to the worker paying the tax via an arcane, complex provision called *the adjustment of the reduction factor* (ARF). The ARF restores, indeed, more than restores, benefits lost to the earnings test. It does so at FRA by permanently raising benefits that have previously been taxed away. Fully understanding Social Security's diabolically cruel pretend labor-income tax can make a huge difference in deciding whether you should work and how much to work if you are below FRA and collecting benefits. If that's not you today, it can be you tomorrow. And if it's not you today or tomorrow, it can be someone you know and like.

Clear as Mud

To see through the retirement trap scam, consider this analogy. Suppose Congress passes a law called the Smith Act. It specifies that anyone whose last name is Smith faces a 100 percent tax on any labor income earned next year. Also assume that Congress meets in a secret session to pass the "Haha, Gotcha Law." The law's first article decrees death by waterboarding for anyone revealing the existence of the law before the end of next year.

The name of the law reflects a terrible practical joke that Congress wishes to play on those named Smith. Why the Smiths? Why not? Congress, in this hypothetical, is nuts—just as nuts as its current 535 members who are retaining the earnings test. Anyway, the "Haha, Gotcha Law" mandates repayment, with interest, at the end of next year of every dollar collected from the Smiths under the Smith Act.

Of course, everyone named Smith, (none of whom hear in time about the "Haha, Gotcha Law" that effectively reverses the Smith Act), does the logical thing. They don't earn a penny next year. They know it will all be taxed away!

At the end of next year, the "Haha, Gotcha Law" is made public—at which point everyone realizes the Smiths were terribly duped. Members of Congress are, as they've been for a year, convulsing with laughter. What a great practical joke! Who cares that many of the Smiths lost their homes, were forced onto the streets, got divorced, became depressed, or perhaps committed suicide during that year without earnings?

Like the Smith Act, the earnings test is a confiscatory tax that isn't. It's a tax that's levied and then secretly returned—costing the government money when measured on an actuarial present value basis. Its sole purpose is to con Social Security beneficiaries below age 67 into thinking that earning money beyond a *de minimus* amount will come at a huge loss in current as well as lifetime benefits. But that's just not true!

The Earnings Test in Social Security's Own Words

In December 2022, I received a letter from Social Security announcing a cost-of-living adjustment (COLA) to my retirement starting in January. An identical letter was sent to all 77 million Social Security beneficiaries. After describing the coming COLA and the impact on federal income tax withholdings, the letter outlines the rules and earnings limit for those working and collecting Social Security at the same time.

Working and Getting Social Security at the Same Time

You can work and still get Social Security benefits. If you are at full retirement age or older, you may keep all your benefits no matter how much you earn. . . . If you are younger than full retirement age at any time in 2023, there is a limit to how much you can earn before we reduce your benefits.

- The 2023 earnings limit for people under full retirement age all year is $21,240. We deduct $1 from your benefits in 2023 for each $2 you earn over $21,240.
- The 2023 earnings limit for people reaching full retirement age in 2023 is $56,520. We deduct $1 from your benefits in 2023 for each $3 you earn over $56,520 until the month you reach full retirement age.

That's the entire description. There is no mention that benefits lost (*reduced* is Social Security's lingo) due to the earnings test are restored, actuarially speaking, at FRA in the form of an inflation-adjusted, permanently higher benefit level. This tax rebate is called the *adjustment of the reduction factor (ARF)*.

Like the "Haha, Gotcha Law," the ARF was designed to restore, down the road, monies lost due to a tax that the government wants people to believe is real. The Congressional Research Service has a well-researched exegesis on the earnings test. As indicated, the earnings test was implemented to punish those perceived to be double dipping—working and collecting benefits. Work or collect, your choice.

The ARF was first implemented in 1961. Until 2000, the earnings test applied through age 70. In that year, President Clinton signed the Senior Citizens Freedom to Work Act, which limited the earnings test to those below FRA.

In other words, the earnings test is a fraud perpetrated on Americans at a vulnerable stage, in the years between age 62 (when they can first collect early Social Security benefits) and roughly age 67, when they reach FRA. Needing the security of a monthly check, too many people opt to take reduced benefits at 62. Then, finding that they cannot make ends meet with their reduced check, they go back to work—desperately trying to stay below the earnings limit (which is far below the poverty level).

Even worse, the ARF overcompensates for benefits lost to the earnings test. The ARF is intended to leave those hit by the earnings test with the same lifetime benefits calculated on an actuarial present value basis. But, in fact, the ARF overcompensates for the tax. That occurs because its actuarial formula was established years ago, when mortality and interest rates were higher. The overcompensation is significant. It means that *almost everyone "taxed" by the earnings test comes out ahead.*

Rather than inform me that I face a massive tax from working if I'm under FRA and collecting, Social Security should inform me that it is subsidizing my working in the weirdest of ways—taking away money now, but giving me significantly more than it is taking away—starting in a few years when I reach full retirement age.

Instead of incentivizing me not to work and not to earn more than the limited amount allowed, the Social Security Administration should be encouraging me to earn a larger paycheck from which FICA would still be deducted. The government would come out ahead, collecting more FICA. I would come out ahead based on the ARF formula. And the economy and America would come out ahead by having a larger, more experienced workforce.

The Duplicitous Language
Underlying This Con Job

The ARF's title is arcane. That's no accident. Like the "Haha, Gotcha Law," the goal of making the ARF indecipherable is doing X without anyone learning you are doing X. If this sounds like another act of intentional deception, you are getting the picture.

The ARF's obscure name and even more obtuse workings were chosen to keep beneficiaries impacted by the earnings test from learning that benefits lost in the short run, based on either a 50 percent or 33 percent marginal tax, would be rebated, indeed overly rebated. These, of course, are fantastically large marginal tax rates—large enough to wipe out every dollar of benefits many younger Social Security beneficiaries receive by returning to work. Again, those lost benefits would be lost for good were it not for the ARF.

Those who know the precise twisted logic underlying the creation of this specific Social Security con job are long gone. But by imposing and maintaining this con for decades, Social Security has led untold millions of early beneficiaries to falsely believe that earning more than a minimum-wage worker is a fool's errand.

The policy works. Various studies, starting, I believe, with this one I authored in 1978, show that early beneficiaries bunch their earnings just below the earnings test thresholds—the levels beyond which benefits are "taxed." No one who understood the ARF would give a fig about the earnings test let alone arrange to earn not a penny more than the threshold amounts (indicated in the above notice) beyond which the earnings test kicks in.

The Cruel Exception

The above sentence is true for almost everyone, but as this boxed description indicates, there is a small subset of people for whom the earnings test is, indeed, a real tax. They are beneficiaries for whom the ARF doesn't help because they will flip to a different benefit at FRA from the one they lost due to the earnings test.

106

When the Earnings Tax Is for Real

An example will clarify. Suppose you are a 62-year-old widow and collecting your retirement benefit. It's low compared to your widow's benefit, which, in your case, maxes out if you collect it at your FRA, which I'll assume is 67. Hence, your optimal strategy is to take your retirement benefit now and your widow's benefit starting at FRA. If you work between 62 and 67 and lose retirement benefits due to the earnings test, the ARF will permanently raise your retirement benefit starting at 67. But that won't compensate you for the lost benefits. Why not? Because you'll flip onto your widow's benefit, which I'm assuming is larger than your retirement benefit even including the ARF. In essence, the short-run tax is more than restored via the ARF but is then confiscated when you take your widow's benefit. To go full nerd, your retirement benefit is increased by the ARF, but your excess widow's benefit is reduced dollar for dollar by the ARF. If you are in this boat, the earnings test is a massive tax on your working between ages 62 and FRA.

The Earnings Test Pretense Lives On

Those who established the pretend tax are no longer alive to admit that the earnings test is a con job. But we can ask senior Social Security officials why they continue, year after year, to run this con. Let me do so right now.

Social Security Commissioner,

Please explain why you are sending out letters that describe the earnings test but not the offsetting ARF. Surely you realize that by falsely telling a 63-year-old beneficiary who is earning above the minimum wage that working full time will place him in a roughly 75 percent tax bracket, once he combines the federal income taxes, FICA taxes, state income taxes, and the earnings test you are conning him out of earning money and, thereby, lowering his current and future living standard. Are you intentionally conning early beneficiaries out of returning to work in order to open up more jobs for younger workers?

Yes, Commissioner, I know this policy isn't of your making. It reflects the Great Depression mentality. But the notices about the earnings test that you are sending out today are indeed of your making. You are fully responsible for the system's communications to the public. And you have a moral, professional, and fiduciary responsibility to tell people the truth.

If you and your staff are too busy to fix your automated notices as well as your website, which is a font of misinformation and missing information, Terry and I will be happy to review and fix your notices, your application forms, and your website content. We'll charge nothing. This work should take, at most, a week.

The True Cost of the Pretend Tax

Let me illustrate the pretend tax, again using Maximize My Social Security. Meet Arthur, a hypothetical age-62, single, never-married Massachusetts resident. Arthur just retired. He was just laid off from his $67,000-paying job because his company lost a major contract.

Short on money, Arthur immediately filed for Social Security. After the reduction for taking his retirement benefit early, Arthur's annual retirement benefit came to $22,226. His lifetime benefits would total $861,213, based on a formula that values benefits through one's maximum age of life.

A year after starting Social Security, Arthur's boss rings him up. The big client has changed its mind. The contract is back on. Could we please rehire you, Arthur?

Arthur, having spent 12 months accumulating blisters bowling with his buddies and failing to improve his game, is desperate to get back to work. But earning $67,000 will, thanks to the earnings test, wipe out all his benefits. Moreover, Arthur will have to pay 15.3 percent of his earnings in payroll taxes since, you will recall, workers pay both the employer and employee halves of the FICA tax despite what Social Security claims. In addition, he will pay 22 percent in federal income taxes, 5 percent in Massachusetts state income taxes, and a disguised labor tax, namely the 6 percent Massachusetts sales tax. (Paying taxes when you use your earnings is fundamentally no different than paying taxes when you receive your earnings.)

When Arthur adds up all these taxes, he realizes he'd be paying almost every penny he'd make to federal and state governments in taxes or lost benefits if he goes back to work.

Arthur, like virtually everyone, never heard of the ARF and the way it actually *returns* benefits lost to the earnings test. Why? Because neither Social Security's commissioner nor his colleagues appreciate their paramount obligation to include this information in bold letters on the Social Security website and in all communications sent to beneficiaries.

Since the Maximize My Social Security software fully incorporates both the earnings test and the ARF, it's easy to see what actually happens to Arthurs benefits if he returns to work and waits till, say, age 67 (his FRA) to start his benefits. Arthur's lifetime benefits rise to $1,045,670. That's a $184,457 increase!

The ARF, as mentioned, more than compensates Arthur for the $86,889 in lifetime benefits he loses to the earnings test.

But something else is going on. By working five more years, Arthur improves his covered earnings record, which further boosts his annual benefit. Thanks to the ARF and Social Security's re-computation of benefits to adjust for those extra earning years, Arthur's inflation-adjusted annual benefit from working through age 67 is $30,190—far above the $22,225 in reduced annual benefits he's now receiving.

Moreover, Arthur's job comes with health insurance. This saves him paying the premiums, through age 65, for an ACA plan. Age 65 is when he would switch to Medicare. Since Arthur will work and be covered at work till 67, he'll also save on premiums for a Medicare Supplement plan. He'll also avoid paying Medicare Parts B and D premiums over the two years.

There are two other winners if Arthur returns to work. Uncle Sam receives more than $50K in present value extra taxes. As for the Commonwealth of Massachusetts, it pulls in an extra $35K in state-income taxes. There's also the extra sales tax the state will collect because of Arthur's increased spending power.

So why does Social Security send Arthur a letter every year between age 62 and 67, reminding him of the huge drop in benefits he will suffer immediately if he goes back to work and earns more than a pittance?

Fixing the Retirement Trap Scam?

Social Security can, for practical purposes, eliminate this scam by clearly and frequently telling early claimants about the ARF. But the real fix is for Congress to simply eliminate the earnings test. Doing so is an economic and fiscal no-brainer.

What about the concern that once people know there is no penalty, they will all take benefits early at age 62, thus losing out on significant lifetime income?

There's a simple answer. It starts with Social Security clearly demonstrating the huge monthly increase to be gained by waiting until at least FRA, or longer. And those who then realize they've made a mistake should have the option to suspend all or a portion of their benefits through FRA, after which they could use the current system that lets you suspend your retirement benefit between FRA and 70.

That would be the fair approach to explaining the impact of taking reduced Social Security benefits before full retirement age. That would be a flexible approach to allowing people to access their benefits, but still have the incentive to return to work and earn necessary income, which will ultimately increase their benefits.

Revealing that there is no actual earnings test would allow Americans to live with the dignity of earned income, while ultimately receiving the full benefits they earned. And it would go a long way toward restoring the integrity of the Social Security system.

That solution is a winner for everyone involved at no additional cost. So, that's our ask: *Stop the retirement trap scam.*

CHAPTER 12

The Contribute-for-Nothing Scam

magine working from, say, age 16 through, say, age 65, paying 12.4 percent of every dollar you earn in FICA taxes, doing so under Social Security's assurance that those contributions will translate into higher retirement benefits, and learning at age 65 that you've been duped. Your Social Security benefits (and, indeed, your Medicare benefits for which you've paid 2.9 percent of every dollar earned) would have been just as high had you never worked a day in your life!

Next, imagine you've paid all of those Social Security taxes, only to meet a neighbor who worked not a minute during his entire life yet is receiving dramatically higher benefits than you.

Welcome to Social Security's contribute-for-nothing scam—pretending that workers' contributions provide higher retirement benefits. This scam impacts workers who receive dependent benefits. They include workers who are married, divorced workers who were married for at least 10 years, and workers who are widowed. If you fit into one of these categories and have or will have low annual earnings or spotty work histories and have a much higher-earning spouse or ex-spouse, you may be victim of the contribute-for-nothing scam.

Victim and scam are strong words for situations in which workers receive nothing in return for years of contributing because they receive higher benefits based on their current spouse's, their dead spouse's, their ex's, or their dead ex's work record. How can getting more than you're owed on your own turn you into a victim?

The answer is that your decisions about working, child care, and much else might have been far different had you known that you would ultimately receive your higher benefits on the work record of your ex-spouse, for example. Thus, all your FICA contributions from your own paycheck actually count for nothing.

For its part, Social Security goes out of its way to make you believe your contributions aren't just an extra tax but represent a form of saving that yields extra future income. Its deception is quite clever—all based on a simple twist of words.

Phantom Retirement Benefits

Social Security's intentionally misleading language pertains to all its benefits. It works like this: If your retirement benefit based on your own work record is $Y, but you are receiving a higher dependent-benefit payment of $X, Social Security will say that you are earning your $Y retirement benefit plus an excess dependent benefit equal to $X–$Y.

When X exceeds Y, Social Security's alternative language works just fine since $X = Y + (X–Y)$, where, again, the second term in parentheses is called your excess dependent benefit. It could be your excess spousal, excess divorced spousal, excess widow(er), or excess divorced widow(er) benefit.

Also note that in contributing more, you raise $Y, your retirement benefit, but don't increase the $X in dependent benefits. The reason is that your excess benefit is reduced dollar for dollar with the increase in $Y. What if Y rises by enough to make X–Y, your excess dependent benefit, negative? In this case, you simply receive your retirement benefit of $Y; i.e., excess benefits can't be less than zero.

This language manipulation avoids Social Security telling everyone in plain English what's going on, namely, If you are eligible to collect a benefit on someone else's record, you'll receive the larger of that benefit and your own retirement benefit. And, in this case, working more to raise your own retirement benefit comes with a 100 percent tax in reducing your excess dependent benefit.

The Costs of This Language Charade

What's the problem, you might ask, in Social Security describing the same outcome with one set of words or another? The answer is that Social Security's language choice disguises the fact that your 12.4 percent-of-pay contributions may be for naught, leaving you, for all intents and purposes, in a 12.4 percentage point higher tax bracket.

Knowing this can lead you to make very different choices. For example, you may decide it's better to stay home with your newborn than enroll the child in an expensive daycare program. Or you might decide to take a far higher, more demanding job to ensure your Social Security contributions pay off. These are all decisions you might make if you understood the true impact on your ultimate Social Security benefits.

Here's an example:

Take Kathy and Jim Jones, both age 30. Kathy is making $30K now and is on a high wage-growth trajectory. When she retires at 62, she'll make close to $125,000 in today's dollars. Jim is pulling in $17K and expects his wages to just keep pace with inflation. When Jim takes Social Security at age 62, his retirement benefit is $12,525 and his excess spousal benefit is $1,333, both in today's dollars. This sums to $13,858.

Jim pays $2,108 annually in FICA taxes. That's $53,263 in lifetime taxes valued in present dollars. It represents over four years of after-tax earnings. What does Jim get in exchange for working 40 hours a week for four years to the exclusive benefit of one party—the Social Security system? The answer is absolutely nothing. He might just as well have been drafted into the army for four years.

To see what's going on, note that were Jim to stop working entirely, his retirement benefit would drop to zero and his excess spousal benefit would rise to $13,858. In short, his retirement benefit comes with a 100 percent tax on his excess spousal benefit.

In raising his retirement benefit by a dollar, he lowers his excess spousal benefit by precisely a dollar. This 100 percent tax on marginal retirement benefits holds for all dependent benefits. If you are collecting or going to collect dependent spousal, ex-spousal, widow(er), or divorced widow(er) benefits, not a penny of your Social Security taxes will impact your future Social Security check when you are collecting those benefits derived from someone else's account.

Does Social Security inform Jim and everyone else that their contributions may provide not a penny more in benefits and that they should regard the FICA tax as a pure tax, no different from the federal income tax? No. Instead, it cons Jim and everyone else into believing that they are receiving the system's generous (at least for low- and moderate-income workers) payback from contributing.

Just look through Social Security's web pages that describe the retirement benefit. Maybe I've missed something, but I've never seen a confession that making Social Security contributions may produce not a penny more in future benefits!

There is one important caveat to what I've just written. By working, Jim receives some protection against disability under the system's disability insurance, or DI program. But Jim's chances of becoming disabled are small. He needs to become disabled to the point where he is unable to do any meaningful work. Even then, he'd likely have a tough time qualifying for benefits.

Half of applicants for disability are denied despite what is often years of appeals. Furthermore, Jim generally needs 40 quarters of work to qualify, with 20 of those quarters earned in the past 10 years. So, he needed to work full time or a full year or even every year to qualify. Also, the average DI benefit is very small—below $1,500 per month.

Most people get their first inkling of this issue when they realize that an ex-spouse (who may never have worked) is collecting benefits on the current spouse's Social Security account. They wonder how the ex can collect, while the current spouse might also collect on higher spousal benefits in the future. Something seems illogical—two (or more) people collecting on the same worker's earnings history.

But if that seems unfair to you, consider how unfair it is to make your own work decisions because you are aiming to collect Social Security benefits on your own account—benefits you will never collect because you may collect via the account of your spouse (or 10-year-ex-spouse).

CHAPTER 13

The Benefit Taxation Scam

H ere's a scam I observed in the making. It involves the law, passed by Congress in 1983, to tax Social Security benefits under the federal income tax. Before then, Social Security benefits were specifically excluded from taxation.

This post-1983 policy operates based on an intentionally highly convoluted formula—one designed to obscure the degree to which our annual Social Security benefits are clawed back, in good measure, every April 15 via the federal income tax. The income tax formula for clawing back benefits we worked our entire lives to accumulate is bad enough. But there's something else about the formula that's far worse, as you'll see.

Income Taxation of Social Security Benefits

Here's how Social Security describes the taxation of Social Security benefits:

> Combined income refers to the sum of adjusted gross income (AGI) plus any nontaxable interest income, plus half of Social Security benefits. AGI includes all standard elements of taxable income, including taxable retirement account withdrawals.

This means, for example, that when we start withdrawing the money that we've saved in our 401(k) plans, those withdrawals can trigger more taxation of our Social Security benefits, meaning the withdrawals will be taxed at a potentially far higher rate than we thought.

> ## Taxation of Social Security Benefits
>
> - File a federal income tax return as an individual and your combined income is
>   - a) between $25,000 and $34,000, you may have to pay income tax on up to 50 percent of your benefits.
>   - b) more than $34,000, up to 85 percent of your benefits may be taxable.
>
> - File a joint return, and you and your spouse have a combined income that is
>   - a) between $32,000 and $44,000, you may have to pay income tax on up to 50 percent of your benefits.
>   - b) more than $44,000, up to 85 percent of your benefits may be taxable.

The Formula

Like everything involving Social Security, you need to think carefully about what's really going on. In the case of benefit taxation, the tax is not so much on Social Security benefits as on your other income.

If you are collecting Social Security, receiving additional taxable income of $X permits making more of your benefit taxable. How much more? Either 50 percent or 85 percent of $X taxable. Even though the additional $X isn't extra Social Security income, it's referred to as $X more of Social Security benefits.

Thus, if you're in, say, the 22 percent tax bracket and the 85 percent Social Security taxation bracket, an extra $1,000 in taxable income means $220 more in taxes on the $1K plus 22 percent of 85 percent of the extra $1,000. In total, the $1K in extra income leads to $407 in extra taxes. You've been pushed from a 22.0 percent marginal tax bracket into a 40.7 percent marginal tax bracket!

There's a limit to this crazy tax. As our combined income keeps rising, maybe because we earn more money or take more taxable withdrawals, we reach the point where the amount of our combined income that exceeds our single or married 85 percent bracket threshold equals the amount of our actual Social Security benefits.

At this point, our taxable income is increased by 85 percent of our actual Social Security benefit and further income increases are taxed at our standard marginal tax bracket rate. Thus, Joe's marginal tax rate, which increases from 22.0 percent to 40.7 percent due to Social Security benefit taxation, reverts back to 22.0 percent.

This crazy pattern of taxation makes deciding when to withdraw your taxable retirement money extremely tough. How much you withdraw this year impacts your tax bracket not just this year, but in every future year as well.

The reason is that higher withdrawals in the present mean lower withdrawals in the future. Figuring out on your own the most tax-efficient pattern of withdrawals would be tough enough without the taxation of Social Security.

Where's the Scam?

Making Social Security benefit taxation so complex is itself a scam—a deliberate decision to confuse people into, perhaps, throwing up their hands and ignoring the issue entirely. Politicians, after all, don't like to be tagged for raising taxes, especially not on their most reliable voters —the elderly.

Whatever the rationale for this byzantine means of taxing benefits, it can put people into far higher marginal tax brackets than they believe they're in. As a result, they can make a host of really bad if not terrible financial decisions. Examples include mistiming their retirement account withdrawals, working overtime for far less after-tax income than they expect, and delaying retirement because they think they're netting more income than is actually the case.

The Real Benefit Taxation Scam

The real scam here is not what we've just described. The real scam is simply not indexing the benefit tax-bracket thresholds to inflation. All other tax brackets in the federal income tax are inflation-indexed, but these are not. This increases the degree of Social Security benefit taxation through time.

Here's the impact: When economies experience inflation, the price of everything rises. This includes the price of labor and the price of borrowing money—interest rates. Consequently, inflation raises taxable income—wages, interest income, and more. Since Social Security benefits are inflation-indexed, they rise as well. As a result, combined incomes rise through time and, since the bracket thresholds are fixed, an ever-larger share of Social Security recipients will find that their combined incomes exceed one or both thresholds.

Eventually, all Social Security beneficiaries will find themselves taxed to the max—on 85 percent of their benefits. Indeed, given that benefits rise with inflation while brackets don't, even those in the future with no other income than Social Security will face taxation of 85 percent of their benefits!

Those getting nailed by this process are, of course, today's middle-aged workers, young workers, children, and all future generations. Do we older generations think our kids and grandkids should pay taxes on 85 percent of their benefits while most of us pay taxes on a far smaller share?

In hiding how this process works, i.e., letting inflation do the dirty work, older generations don't likely even realize their children are being gradually expropriated out of a goodly share of their future Social Security income.

This Scam Was Carefully Designed

Secretly letting inflation tax future Social Security recipients to ever-higher brackets was the brainchild of David Stockman, President Reagan's budget director. I attended a meeting in the Old Executive Office Building in the spring of 1982 in which David (we now know each other enough to be on a first name basis) was crowing about the manner in which he established his new scheme for clawing back benefits from young and future generations.

To give David his due, he was deeply concerned about our nation's long-term fiscal insolvency. Social Security's finances would certainly be in far worse shape absent the taxation of benefits. Yet I was, and remain, appalled by the policy and its intergenerational inequity.

David's technique was to propose a package of Social Security policies to Congress, several of which would almost surely be rejected out of hand. But others would slip through as the public's attention was diverted. His top loss leader was cutting early retirement benefits immediately, meaning those about to collect benefits would be very badly hurt.

David said he knew this proposal would go down in flames. The vote was, I believe, 100 to 0 against in the Senate. But, as David confidentially told us, his goal was to plant a fiscal poison pill: not indexing the Social Security taxation brackets, thereby increasing the tax burden on beneficiaries over time. The increased taxes raised have certainly helped the system's finances, but is terribly unfair to future generations.

I hadn't voted for President Reagan and was almost fired four times during my time on the Council—not for insubordination, but for insisting we tell the full truth about the Reagan Revolution's policies—the bad as well as the good. That story is for another day. The point here is that David and the members of Congress who ultimately adopted Social Security benefit taxation absent indexation knew what they were doing in adopting the policy. Successive Congresses have also known what they are doing in continuing to leave the tax thresholds fixed in nominal dollars.

CHAPTER 14

The Take-Your-Benefits-Early Scam

learned about this scam in a dentist's chair. The dentist, Dr. Stanley, wasn't someone I generally see. He was giving me Botox injections for TMJ (jaw clenching). I figured he was in his seventies. I had just written my co-authored book, *Get What's Yours: The Secrets to Maxing Out Your Social Security.*

The book, which remains fully up to date, became a best seller. It was #1 on the *NY Times* best seller list for 10 days and on its top-10 list for over nine months. It's crazy that a book about Social Security rules could attract so much attention. But my co-authors, Paul Solman of *PBS NewsHour* and Phil Moeller, a longtime personal finance columnist, then with U.S. News, are very funny people.

Anyway, the doc had heard of the book and asked me about it. I, in turn, asked what Social Security decisions he'd made.

I took my benefit at 70. Actually, I took it at 69 and a half. A lady called me from Social Security and said I could start immediately. They'd even give me six months benefits retroactively. I was surprised and delighted. I took the deal. I had no idea you could take your highest benefit early and get a six-month bonus in the process.

I groaned internally but held my tongue. Dr. Stanley was heading my way, long needle in hand. But, a few minutes later, before receiving the bill, I deflated Dr. Stanley's bubble.

I'm really sorry to tell you this, but Social Security scammed you. This is the first time I've heard of this practice. But I'm not entirely surprised. I've heard so many terrible things done by the staff over the years. Here's what happened. They set your retirement benefit filing date back to age 69. Then they gave you a half year's benefit since you had, according to them, started your benefit on your 69th birthday. The money they gave you wasn't a bonus. It was just your permanently reduced benefit for months it hadn't been paid.

In electing to take your benefit at 69, you gave up what you were trying to do, namely wait till 70 and accrue another year of delayed retirement benefits. That would have meant an 8 percent higher monthly benefit. Didn't they tell you this in the conversation? They never said that doing what they suggested was going to lower your retirement benefit by 8 percent for the rest of your life?

Dr. Stanley, whose assistant was off for the day, was writing out the bill for my uninsured procedure. His face was now deep red. I was sure he was going to shoot the messenger. Here's what he said as he handed me the bill:

What do you mean I elected to take my benefit at 69? They never suggested any such thing. I told them I was waiting till 70 to collect and they said they could start my benefit right away and give me a six-month bonus.

Now my face was reddening. The bill was a good 50 percent higher than expected.

I'm really sorry I brought this up, but I thought you should know that you were scammed by our own government. Maybe it was an overzealous staff member or local office run by someone who thinks people should take their benefits early and not risk dying too late to get them.

The doctor, who had, he told me, read my book, replied:

That's stupid. It's covered in chapter one in your book. You can't count on dying on time. The real danger is not dying without having collected. Financially, your bills stop. You don't need money if you die. I've never heard you need money in the hereafter. Maybe in purgatory, but surely not in heaven. This is so discouraging. It's enough for me to switch to the Libertarian Party.

By now, I'm walking out the door. But I turn back and say:

If this was a year after receipt of your hitting 69, you could formally withdraw your benefit and refile at 70. But it's beyond a year. Please don't take this too hard. Yes, you were scammed. But that's Social Insecurity for you.

Is This Scam Ongoing?

After leaving my dentist office, I contacted someone senior at Social Security about what I'd heard and how it had cost me an extra $150. My contact there said, "We can't be doing this. I'll check into it."

The checking into it seems not to have mattered. I've heard of five to ten more cases of people getting the call and the so-called bribe. For all I know, this is happening every day across the country—Social Security preying on people in their late sixties who they know are trying to maximize their benefit to provide maximum protection against old age.

Why was the system doing this and, I presume, still doing it? It's been a bit since anyone reported to me that they had been so approached. Maybe the practice has been stopped, but I doubt it. It would require writing over 60 thousand staff around the country that the practice has been going on and needs to stopped. If it were to leak out, it might end up producing a class-action suit. Meanwhile, I've stopped seeing Dr. Stanley. I no longer trust him with that needle.

CHAPTER 15

The Crazy Calculator Scam

oogle "Social Security benefit calculators" and you'll come to its Quick Calculator. You can also log into your My Social Security account and use its online calculator. Social Security also has a detailed downloadable calculator.

Establishing a My Social Security account is quite the ordeal. Here's the email I received last night from Terry when she tried to get into her own account as we were working on this book project. Her subject line was, "I'm still shaking."

Hi Larry,

Just got off the phone with SS re my own account. (Remember, I wanted to follow up to get my earnings record). I was on hold for 53 minutes.

I had my previous log-in information (user name/password) and I tried several times over 3 days. They recognized me but said they needed to send me a confirming email with a code to enter.

That email never came—and I tried at least 4 times. Yes, checked my spam. So, I decided to call.

Finally, after nearly an hour got a guy to help. He confirmed all my information (birth date, city, mother's maiden name, etc.) He suggested I request a new password. So, I did. Then it asked me three personal questions, which I answered correctly.

And then it led me back to the SAME page, telling me they would send an email with a code. Of course, it never came.

His suggestion: start over with a new account and a new email. I told him I didn't have another email!

Next suggestion: they will MAIL me a temporary password, good for 30 days. I will wait for it!!

Finally, I said that since I had him on the line, could he explain why I was receiving no increase in benefits—except inflation adjustments—even though I continued to work.

I explained that every single year for 35 years, I had earned beyond the earnings cap. But every year the earnings cap had increased! So now that I have all these additional years of earnings over the HIGHER CAP, why haven't my benefits increased?

He gave me so much mumbo-jumbo and got angry when I pressed him.

He said earnings after age 70 don't count towards the 35-year calculation of benefits.

He said earnings OVER each year's cap don't count.

He said a higher cap doesn't impact the calculation of 35 years of benefits.

Is that true? I honestly didn't know. This isn't for the book— but I'd really like to know if he is correct!

And it gave me a true lesson in patience! And some more advice for our readers!

A Strict Lesson from One Phone Call— *Never Ask Social Security Staff Anything*

We're going to get back to Social Security's calculators in a moment. But let's take stock of Terry's experience. Unfortunately, it's standard.

No one I know has been able to get ready access to their My Social Security account. It took me multiple tries over a week and I finally succeeded. Who knows how many people have given up.

But what about Terry's question? Did the Social Security staffer give her correct information? Two out of three things he said are completely wrong. The third is incomplete and misleading. Let's review.

He said that earnings after age 70 don't count towards the 35-year calculation of benefits.

Wrong. They do count. Every year's earnings count in determining what are the highest 35 years of earnings. Those earnings that arise before age 60 are indexed using the economy-wide average wage index to account for growth in this index through the year you reach age 60.

After age 60, your nominal (actual dollar) earnings are ranked together with your pre-age-60 indexed earnings as well as your age 60 earnings to determine your highest 35 values. These values are then divided by 35 times 12 to form your *average indexed monthly earnings* (AIME). Your AIME value is the basis for determining your full retirement benefit or PIA (primary insurance amount).

You could be 90 and still be raising your AIME and, thus, your PIA because your nominal earnings at 90 exceed one of the other previously highest 35 wage values. If you raise your AIME, you'll raise your PIA, meaning your benefits will rise come January 1 by more than the COLA. This is called Social Security's re-computation of benefits.

The only reason your monthly check/deposit won't increase is if you are receiving a dependent benefit. In this case, as described above, your excess dependent benefit will be reduced dollar for dollar due to the increase in your retirement benefit arising from the re-computation of benefits.

He said that earnings over each year's cap don't count.

Ok, but what he should have added is that if you earn above the cap, you are guaranteed, given that wage indexation ends at 60, to have a higher AIME and, thus, receive a higher retirement benefit apart from the COLA. Again, this assumes you aren't receiving an excess dependent benefit.

He said that a higher cap doesn't impact the calculation of 35 years of benefits.

Wrong. He needs to read my co-authored book, *Get What's Yours: The Secrets to Maxing Out Your Social Security*. Apparently, his training didn't include the basics. In particular, he didn't learn how benefits are actually calculated. Or he learned and then forgot. That's understandable. The details are as dull as paint.

But a higher cap means that those who earn this year near or at or over the cap will absolutely replace a lower-earning year with this year's cap in determining the highest 35 values. The reason is that the highest your earnings can be prior to age 60 is the age-60 cap value. And caps after age 60 are always higher than at age 60.

Can You Access Social Security's Calculators?

Good question. Unlike Terry, I can log into my Social Security account. Theoretically, I should be able to find the advanced online calculator to check how much working in the future will raise my benefit above and beyond inflation—due to Social Security's annual re-computation of benefits. I can find no such calculator. This may reflect the fact that I'm already collecting; i.e., Social Security may have turned off the calculator for people like me thinking we don't know enough to check how extra earnings will raise our benefits.

My inability to access the online calculator leaves me with two options—use its online Quick Calculator (as in quick and dirty) or download the Detailed Calculator. The extensive directions for installing this *Anypia* tool on a Mac conclude with this statement: "Note that this Mac version will not work on a Mac running Lion or newer versions of the OS X operating system. We hope to produce a Mac version which will work on newer versions of OS X, but we have very limited resources to devote to that project at this time."

Unfortunately, I have a modern Mac so this was strike two. I headed over the Social Security's Quick Calculator. Here I confirmed what I learned years back. This calculator makes the completely insane assumption that our economy will never experience future inflation or economy-wide wage growth.

In fact, inflation has been crazy high the last two years and is still running at 4 percent. And average wage growth is starting to keep pace. Plus, you can count in one or two fingers the number of postwar years that inflation and average wage growth have been zero or slightly negative. If these assumptions didn't matter to the calculator's benefit projection it would be one thing. But they matter dramatically.

Why assume an alien economic world? The answer, which I was told by someone quite senior in Social Security, is that the system wants to lowball workers' future benefit estimates to scare them into saving more on their own. Here, again, we encounter Social Security's ingrained problem in telling the truth.

The lowballing is greater the younger you are. I ran a case of a single 40-year-old through the Quick Calculator and Maximize My Social Security (MMSS). In running *MMSS*, I assumed we'll have 2.25 percent inflation over the long term—what the market is predicting. *MMSS* assumes, consistent with the 2023 Trustees Report, that real (inflation-adjusted) wages will grow at 1.63 percent per year. In both runs, I assumed the worker would start collecting at age 62 and that his wages would remain fixed at $75K in today's dollars through retirement.

The head-to-head comparison was striking. Social Security's Quick Calculator underestimated the 40-year-old's age-62 benefit by 24 percent! That's a massive mistake.

What if the person were, say, 63 and still working? The Quick Calculator will potentially overstate his benefit by assuming he'll work till FRA, namely 67. You can modify these earnings inputs if you click around and find the right link. But since you can't tell the program about your spouse's, ex-spouse's, dead spouse's, or dead ex-spouse's earnings record, *the* Quick Calculator and the other tools may tell you about retirement benefits you'll effectively never receive.

Before we end this chapter, Terry is still waiting for the promised letter that will get her access to her account. And still wondering why her check has not increased (after reviewing my answer above). Shouldn't Social Security recalculate those benefits every year for the impact of continued earnings? And shouldn't it disclose any increase, or let you know why—despite continuing to earn the cap amount—the check remains unchanged, except for the COLA??

In the beginning of this book we noted that Social Security makes huge mistakes in overpayments, then claws back its own errors? We wondered about potential underpayments. This is likely one of those cases.

CHAPTER 16

The Employer Contribution Scam

G oogle "FICA taxes." You'll find a Social Security web page entitled "What Is FICA?" It offers a graphic suitable for a 12-year-old that says:

> "FICA is a U.S. federal payroll tax. It stands for the Federal Insurance Contributions Act and is deducted from each paycheck. 6.2 percent of your gross wages goes to Social Security tax and 1.45 percent of your gross wages goes to Medicare tax.*"

It looks like a relatively small percentage "contribution." But don't overlook that asterisk. It leads you to the smaller print which says: *"Your employer matches these percentages for a total contribution of 15.3 percent."*

Well, isn't that a lovely thing for your employer to do. Year and year out, in good times and bad, your employer makes a 6.2 percent contribution on your behalf out of the goodness of its heart. The only problem with this fairytale is that it's another Social Security deception.

Employers aren't our friends. They aren't our parents. They aren't even our ninth cousins twenty-times removed. They hire us for one reason only—to make money. And they pay us based on our contribution to their bottom line. If that's $25 an hour, i.e., $1,000 a month, they are happy to pay us $1,000 per month, but not a penny more. And they are happy to pay these funds in in any way we or Uncle Sam directs.

You can say:

Each month, please send me $915 and Aunt Ida $85 a month. Please send both amounts by direct deposit.

Or you can say:

Of my $1,000 monthly earnings, keep sending Ida the $85. Please also send the IRS $250 for federal income taxes; send $100 to my state's department of revenue for state income taxes; send the IRS $153 for Social Security and Medicare taxes FICA. Split the $153 into two pieces. Send one wire for $76.50 with the notation "employee contribution" and the other for $76.50 with the notation "employer contribution."

The IRS wants you to send the $153 in one lump sum, so you call them and explain that they must record that half is the employee and half is the employer contribution. However, IRS cares just about the total, so you describe the full $153 as just an employer contribution.

You explain that you would prefer not to pay any FICA taxes.

I know that what you send Ida and the IRS in total comes straight out of the $1,000 per month, but I like the sound of getting Social Security and Medicare benefits for nothing even if it's completely untrue. Plus, call the monthly $153 'FICA contribution' not 'FICA taxes.' I hate taxes.

As I'm thinking about it, I realize that I have no idea what my extra contributions will produce in present value extra Social Security benefits. If I'm going to collect as a dependent of someone else, the answer is zero. Also, I realize the system is dead broke. I realize my payments are going right out the door to keep our national Ponzi scheme running. I realize those running our great national chain letter will likely change the law and I'll get peanuts back on the dollar.

I may be gullible, but I'm not an idiot. I know the PIA formula is highly progressive, so that my extra "'contributions' aren't yielding much in extra benefits. Also, I realize that $29 of the $153, is supposedly for Medicare benefits. But I've already contributed enough quarters to earn those benefits, so the monthly $29 doesn't produce a penny more of anything.

But, still, do call it all a contribution. Indeed, call every penny you send to the Feds and my state government a contribution. Why not? I hate paying taxes. And the politicians hate admitting they are charging me taxes. So, let's use phony words that make everyone feel better, but have no impact on my bottom line—what I end up getting to spend.

If I'm so blasé about making contributions, for no clear payback, am I willing to contribute more than $153 for nothing? Of course not. I'm in deep denial, but not that deep.

We have, by now, hammered home the point. Describing half our FICA Social Security payments as "contributions" that our benevolent employers are fully matching, rather than acknowledging that they are reducing our take-home pay dollar for dollar, is part and parcel of the worst Social Security story going—hiding our great, national Ponzi scheme from clear sight.

CHAPTER 17

Social Security's Sexism Scam

Social Security's dependent-benefit rules were written in the fifties, sixties, and seventies. They were written by high-income men. Why men? Because the people who wrote these rules were some combination of members of Congress, congressional lawyers, and Social Security staff, particularly the commissioner and chief actuary. None of them, back then, were women.

Back then, women were supposed to "know their place,"—stay at home, clean the house, shop for essentials, make supper, bring up the kids, remain monogamous, and, in the case of divorce, not remarry.

For women who misbehave, the rules provided and still provide (since they remain fully in place) significant penalties. As for new wives, the rules were and are very generous. This is particularly true of younger new wives marrying high-income older men. The men who wrote those rules knew how to enhance their attraction should they find themselves single late in life.

De Jure Versus De Facto Treatment

Facially, Social Security is sex-neutral. That wasn't always the case. Early on, the program made it easier for widows to collect on their deceased husbands or ex-husbands. But a Supreme Court decision in 1977 made Social Security legally sex-neutral. The Court ruled that any sex-based distinction in Social Security provisions violated the Fifth Amendment's due process clause.

Hence, our claim that Social Security is incredibly and intentionally sexist is not due to the letter of its law. Rather it's due to two main

135

factors—eligibility provisions affecting divorcées and the way the system treats spouses who are secondary earners, the majority of whom were and are women.

Wives' labor force participation is far lower than that of husbands in general, but particularly when children are young. In addition, working women continue, as has been the case for decades, to earn almost one-fifth less than working men. It's no surprise then that, in over half of marriages, men are the primary or sole breadwinner.

Let's now turn to Social Security's sexist provisions. But, in so doing, turn back the clock to, say, 1960, when husbands were the primary or sole breadwinners in virtually all marriages. This will help you understand what the men writing these rules were after.

We understand that times have changed, but they have not changed that much. Moreover, for any current married female who stays home to care for her children, nothing has changed. The system's sexism is as pronounced for her as it was in 1960. Of course, sexism describes discrimination of an entire gender. We view Social Security as sexist because its rules are more likely to harm women than men.

Finally, in considering the following sexist provisions, realize that they all involve dependent benefits written by males who, in the main, envisioned their wives not as independent of them, but as dependent on them. Had they not wished to use Social Security to make wives more dependent on husbands, they could easily have credited half of a married couple's combined covered earnings to each spouse. This would have obviated the supposed need for dependent benefits because divorce or death of the higher earning male would not have left nonworking or low-earning women so greatly in need of dependent benefits to help sustain their living standards.

You Need to Be Married for 10 or More Years to Collect Divorcée Spousal or Divorcée Widow Benefits

Joe and Cindy are a married hypothetical Texas couple with three kids. Joe's the sole breadwinner. Like half of today's married couples—the half that end up getting divorced—Joe and Cindy don't get along. Truth be told, Joe has been seeing Sandy. But when Cindy starts to date Sam, Joe gets angry and threatens divorce. He believes infidelity should go in one direction.

Texas provides for child support, but is awful when it comes to mandating decent levels and durations of alimony payments. Cindy's petrified of becoming bereft of income. Here, Joe, who wants to keep his options open if Sandy doesn't work out, holds all the cards plus a Social Security trump card.

Joe tells Cindy, "If I divorce you, your alimony will be peanuts. Plus, I'll make sure to time the divorce well before or right before we've been married for 10 years. This way, you'll have no claim whatsoever on future Social Security benefits based on my earnings record."

Joe's got it right. In order to be eligible to collect divorcée spousal or divorcée widow's benefits you need to be married for 10 or more years.

If you divorce nine years and 364 days after getting married, your claim to benefits based on your ex's work record goes poof. With one in three marriages ending in divorce before 10 years, secondary earners need to look out. Yes, a couple can separate and wait 10 years to get divorced. Indeed, they can live at opposite ends of the earth and will still be viewed as married by Social Security.

But either spouse can force the other spouse to get divorced well before a decade is up—perhaps, to remarry or perhaps to cut the spouse out of any claim to divorcée benefits. This second objective reflects pure spite. Divorcée benefits don't impact a worker's own benefits or those of future wives and children one iota.

What's sexist here? Potential divorcée benefit claimants are primarily nonworking moms caring for their kids. Social Security's 10-year requirement for divorcée benefits gives the higher-earning spouse, typically the husband, potentially huge coercive powers over his wife.

This power of one spouse over the other applies to any married couple when one spouse earns substantially more than the other and when the lower-earning spouse is also a lifetime low earner. The average monthly excess spousal benefit of married or divorced spouses is close to $1,000. That's peanuts for most households, but a fortune for someone with very little, if any, other income.

Divorced? Say Goodbye to Child-in-Care
Spousal Benefits Unless You're Older Than 62

This rule is particularly useful to scare young, nonworking moms into sticking with their disabled or older husbands. In the case of husbands who are receiving disability or retirement benefits, the nonworking mom can collect a child-in-care spousal benefit.

The only requirement is that the couple's child or children be young (under 18 or 19, but still in high school) or disabled. Due to the family benefit maximum—a rule limiting total dependent benefits that can be collected on a worker's record, the size of the child-in-care benefit will depend on how many children are collecting child or disabled child benefits.

All very nice. But if the mom wants out of the marriage via divorce, she'll lose her child-in-care benefit, however large it is, even though she's still caring for her ex's, as well as her own, children. To add insult to injury, if the ex remarries and the kids move in with dad, the step-mom can collect what would have been the real mother's child-in-care benefits!

Remarry After Getting Divorced?
Say Goodbye to Divorcée Spousal Benefits

Many states tell divorcées that their alimony payments will end if they remarry. Maybe this makes sense if the recipient marries someone wealthy. But the rule applies to all divorcées. Since males typically earn more than females and earned lots more when these alimony provisions were either adopted formally, through legislation, or infor-mally, via standard family judge rulings, this lets higher-earning hus-bands convey this message to their wives about divorce: "Your choice, but I get to cut you off if you remarry."

Social Security contributes to this nasty remarriage tax by ending divorcée spousal benefits the month a divorced spouse remarries. To collect divorcée spousal benefits, there are lots of catch 22s. You had to have been married for at least a decade. Your ex must be at least 62. You must be divorced for at least two years unless your ex is collecting his retirement benefit. And you must be at least age 62.

In any case, it's a nasty piece of work hanging over the heads of all divorced wives who qualify or would qualify for a divorced spousal benefit. It's a way for husbands to control wives decades after they got divorced. It tells many wives—"Listen, if you divorce me, I'll not only stop paying you alimony regardless of your age. I'll also enlist Social Security to keep you from collecting a penny on my work record while I'm alive."

If You Are Divorced After a 10-Year Marriage and Your Ex Dies, You Can Collect a Child-in-Care Divorced Spousal Benefit, but Only After Reaching Age 62

Here, again, we have an instance of punishing a divorcée who is caring for her child and likely in need of support. When the ex of a 10-year or longer marriage is alive, the divorcée can't collect. But somehow it's ok for her to collect once the ex dies, provided she is 62 or older. Treating an older divorcée different from a younger divorcée is, it seems, intended to deprive the divorcée of resources when she is young and has retained her looks. Once she has reached 62, her likelihood of connecting with someone new is, the authors of this rule surely presumed, lower. Hence, there is less chance that this benefit would be shared with a new male. This represents financial control beyond the grave. And it's still fully on the books!

Remarry Before 60?
Lose Your Right to Divorcée Widow Benefits

Here, too, we have a presumed angry male divorcé, not satisfied with his ex having spent at least 10 likely unhappy years with him, making sure that she can't share his benefits derived from his work record unless she is old enough to have limited remarriage prospects. This is jealousy from the grave.

Laws can be changed from one day to the next. Hence, the fact that this provision is retained year after year means that the current powers that be think it's appropriate. In this case, they should explain why they are imposing this, practically, not legally, speaking, sexist provision with its peculiar age limit.

The reality is that of our 535 members of Congress, not a single member is likely aware of this provision. And if asked to explain it, they would baffled. But they would likely also realize that the age limit has some connection to the dependent divorcée's attractiveness and ability to remarry.

Nonworking Wives Can Receive Higher Benefits Than Working Wives If They Marry Rich

This is the "contribute for nothing" scam discussed in Chapter 12. Take two wives, A and B. They both have high-earning husbands who earn the same amount. Wife A doesn't work a day in her life and pays not a penny in Social Security taxes. Wife B works every day of her life and pays 12.4 percent of every dollar she earns to Social Security.

Wife A and wife B can collect exactly the same benefits, i.e., wife B may get absolutely nothing back in return for paying FICA taxes month after month, year after year on every penny she earns. Next suppose wife A's husband earns more than wife B's. In this case, wife A can end up with more benefits than wife B even though she hasn't paid a penny into the system.

The scam, to repeat, involves telling wife B that she is earning her own retirement benefit and not telling her that every dollar increase in her retirement benefit comes with a dollar reduction in her excess spousal, excess divorced spousal, excess widow, or excess divorced widow benefit provided she is entitled to collect those benefits.

For wives, including divorced wives, who are in this boat and understand the system, this excess benefit tax places them in a 12.4 percent higher effective marginal tax bracket. Their total tax bracket—their combined work disincentive—is also determined by their federal and state income tax brackets.

For married women, particularly those married to high-earning men, the incentive to work will be small enough as it is. Since they will surely be filing a joint tax return, they will, thanks to their husband's earnings, be in a high tax bracket even ignoring the FICA tax.

But unlike their assumed higher-earning husbands whose extra FICA contributions come with potentially higher benefits not just for themselves, but for their wives and children, the extra FICA taxes paid by dependent wives deliver no extra benefits. This is nicely designed to keep the women of high-earning men at home, taking care of the couple's children, not meeting other men at work with whom they might have an affair or run off, and not establishing a career on which they can rely if they divorce.

Ex-Husbands Can Control Dependent Wives' and Ex-Wives' Benefits by Earning Less, Retiring Early, or Taking Their Retirement Benefits Early

Excess dependent spousal benefits paid to wives or ex-wives depend on the full retirement age benefit of the current or former husband. He has the potential ability to lower those benefits by reducing his covered earnings by working less in a given year or simply quitting work.

Depending on his prior covered earnings history, this will reduce his FRA benefit, which is used in calculating his wife's excess spousal and excess divorced spousal benefit. As for excess widow's and divorced widow's benefits, each depends on the actual benefit the decedent husband or dead ex was receiving when he died. A decision by the current or ex-hubby to file for retirement benefits early is a decision to reduce those survivor benefits.

Thus, for many current and divorced husbands, taking retirement benefits early, retiring early, and earning less prior to retirement are three potent means of extracting revenge on a former wife who they once vowed to protect and defend and now can't wait to undermine and injure, as least financially.

A Wife Can't Collect Her Spousal Benefit until Her Husband Files for His Retirement Benefit, Which Can Be as Late as His Reaching Age 70

Another means of keeping one's low-earning (in absolute and relative terms) wife under one's thumb is to keep her from collecting her excess spousal benefit by waiting till age 70 to collect your retirement benefit. To be clear, this may be in the wife's best lifetime benefit interest because it maximizes her potential widow's benefit.

In many households, the person who receives the income determines who gets to spend and on what. Dependent benefits paid on a worker's earnings record are only available if the worker either files for his retirement benefit or dies. This said, wives are free to file for their own retirement benefit as early as 62. In some cases, they should start collecting their own retirement benefit before their husband starts his. Otherwise, they will simply leave money on the table. Maximize My Social Security will clarify what to do if you are in this boat.

A Divorced Wife, Married for a Decade-Plus, Must Wait Until Her Ex Is 62 and She Has Been Divorced for Two-Plus Years Unless Her Over-62 Ex Has Filed for His Retirement Benefit

If a divorced wife is 62 and her ex is 42, this provision requires her to wait till age 82 to file for divorced spousal benefits. This provision was, we guess, adopted to keep older women from gold digging benefits from younger males. But these supposed gold diggers would have to have stayed married for a decade to someone they intended to divorce. So, if this is the explanation for this bizarre requirement, it makes little sense. It more likely reflects males feeling unfairly treated if their exes get to start benefits before they do.

The two-year waiting period is another nasty sexist piece of work. It means, for example, that a 62-year-old wife who divorces her 62-year-old husband after, say, 25 years of marriage has to wait till age 64 to file for her divorced spousal benefit. Where is this coming from except as a means of punishing the wife?

Delayed Retirement Credits Are Not Provided to Spouses or Divorced Spouses for Waiting Beyond Full Retirement Age to Collect Their Excess Spousal or Divorced Spousal Benefits

Delayed retirement credits (DRCs) are available to workers if they wait beyond FRA to start their retirement benefit. The DRCs equal 8/12 percent per month or 8 percent per year. Hence, if an ex-husband with an age 67 FRA waits till 70 to start his retirement benefit, the benefit will start 24 percent (3 years times 8 percent per year) higher than had he started it at 67. The 8 percent per year size of DRCs is extremely generous—so generous that roughly 90 percent of workers should wait till age 70 to start their retirement benefit if they seek to maximize lifetime benefits.

But this substantial advantage to waiting is not provided to either spouses or ex-spouses. Why not? Maybe the males who established DRCs were older? And maybe these males who established DRCs were in an economic position to wait till 70 to begin collecting retirement benefits? And maybe these older, financially liquid older males who invented DRCs did so to help themselves to substantially higher lifetime benefits?

All of these maybes appear to be certainties. The average age of senators in 1972, when delayed retirement credits were first enacted, was well above 50. House members were younger. But the chairmen of the key congressional committees that implemented DRCs were considerably older than average because they attained their posts by accumulating seniority.

Wives, Including Ex-Wives Who Are Three or More Years Younger Than Their Husbands, Never Have to Wait Beyond Full Retirement Age to Collect Full Spousal Benefits

One feature of Social Security's disguised de facto sexism is that it treats younger wives better than older ones. As indicated, eligible wives can't collect their excess spousal benefits before their husbands start collecting their own retirement benefits. Since the latest the husband will wait is age 70 and since the system's full retirement age is rapidly reaching age 67, any wife who is three or more years younger than her husband and is able to collect an excess spousal benefit will, when reaching FRA, never be forced to wait to start that benefit and will start it on an unreduced basis.

Because They Accumulate Less Wealth Prior to Reaching Age 62, Women Are Less Likely Than Men to Be Able to Afford to Wait to Collect Higher Benefits

Waiting beyond full retirement age and, for most workers, waiting till age 70 to start their retirement benefits is enormously valuable for two reasons. First, not taking your retirement benefit before FRA means it won't be actuarially reduced. Second, waiting beyond FRA provides significant actuarial increases via the acquisition of delayed retirement credits.

For historical reasons the system's actuarial reductions for taking benefits early, before FRA, are far greater than actuarially fair. And the increases for waiting to take benefits after FRA are far larger than are actuarially fair.

The upshot of these two features is that workers who delay taking their retirement benefit until age 70 receive an inflation-adjusted benefit—a benefit measured in today's dollars—that is 76 percent higher than had they started their benefit at age 62. Age 62 is, recall, the earliest age at which one can start collecting retirement benefits.

Husbands Can Quickly Secure Spousal and Widow's Benefits for New Wives

The waiting periods for eligibility to collect excess spousal and excess widow's benefits are only 12 months and 9 months, respectively. This means an older male with a significant earnings record can entice a younger, low-earning female to marry with the assurance of substantial future Social Security benefits.

Indeed, if the couple has young or disabled children, the wife will be eligible to collect child-in-care spousal benefits while the husband is alive. And if her husband passes, she'll also be able to collect mother benefits—benefits available to mothers of deceased spouses who are caring for the young or disabled children of their deceased husbands.

Consider a 90-year-old male with a three-year life expectancy seeking to marry a 67-year-old female for companionship and old-age care. Also suppose the male is receiving today's maximum annual retirement benefit of $54,660.

Then his young wife-to-be can expect, within a couple of years, to receive that income for the rest of her days, on an inflation-adjusted basis, by saying "I do" and by keeping her husband alive for at least nine months. Note that if the husband dies for unexpected medical reasons, like having a heart attack on their wedding night, Social Security can waive the nine-month marriage duration rule.

Summing Up

Social Security's above 13 sexist features could, of course, be viewed as discriminating against males rather than females if males rather than females were the primary caregivers to children and if male and female earnings distributions were the reverse of what we observe. But the world is what it is, and Social Security's sexist provisions were established and are being maintained by Congress year after year knowing the asymmetric positions of males and females.

PART 3

Avoiding Your Personal and Our Collective Social Security Horror Stories

CHAPTER 18

Don't Trust
Social Security

arry has heard one awful story after another about Social Security misinformation. He's also sampled it firsthand. He recalls a 2018 case involved an early retiree—we'll call him Ben—seeking to suspend his retirement benefit at full retirement age and restart it at 70 at a roughly 30 percent higher real level. MMSS calculated this as Ben's lifetime benefit optimizing strategy. But when Ben went to his local office, the claims rep told him that suspending benefits had been disallowed three years earlier with the 2015 changes to the law.

Ben contacted MMSS customer support and was assured that the software was correct and that the agent was wrong. Larry heard about the case and asked Ben to set up a call with the agent—a call he would join. (Social Security permits claimants to have advocates attend meetings.)

This actual Social Security staffer was intensely hostile and aggressive. The conversation began as follows: "I've been working here for 14 years. I know all the regs inside and out. You are, let me get this straight, a professor? You really think you can tell me how to do my job? Your software is horribly wrong."

The staffer's voice rose and so did the rapidity of her words and the intensity of her disdain. After three minutes, Larry couldn't get a word in edgewise. Her rant lasted a half hour. That was plenty of time to check the relevant sections of Social Security's Program Operating Manual System that Larry had provided. As the half-hour rant drew to a close, the staffer came up for air and asked Larry if he had any questions.

He did. He asked her to confirm her name, office address, and supervisor's name to ensure they appeared correctly in the *Forbes* article he had been writing as she had been screaming. He said it would be posted in a half hour.

The staffer abruptly hung up.

Fifteen minutes later, Larry's phone rang. It was the staffer calling to apologize. She had checked with her supervisor. She had been wrong. Would Larry please excuse her and ignore their exchange? He said, "Of course" and thanked her for checking.

Treat Social Security as your Adversary

There are myriad ways Social Security can screw up your benefit calculation leading to under- or overpayments. First, it may fail to correctly credit your past covered earnings, starting from age 16 on. Second, its computer system can go haywire. Third, it lacks—for many people—vital information to accurately calculate their benefits. Fourth, its staff may file you for benefits you didn't request. Fifth, its staff may input incorrect information into its system. Sixth, Social Security is not immune from hacks. And seventh, the staff can give you terrible advice.

Frequently, the errors made by Social Security in calculating your benefits result from a combination of those factors. But you will never know they made a mistake until they finally contact you, demanding money. And if you have been *under*paid over your lifetime, you might never know how much money you left on the table.

Protecting yourself means having all the data you need to figure out what you should be receiving currently and through time. And it means knowing the fundamentals of how the system works so you can check that you're being treated properly.

After reading hundreds of Social Security horror stories sent to us, one thing is clear: Social Security preys on the most vulnerable. Contacting Social Security in tears and fear, without a base of knowledge and some confidence in your position, seems to trigger a predator response in many claims representatives.

So let us help you defend yourself against Social Security. Ignorance is not bliss! And Social Security is not your friend.

As we've learned from a senior Social Security attorney who worked for years with the agency and has many internal contacts, the system's culture has changed. Three decades back, the goal was "make every effort to process a claim." Today the goal seems to be: "deny as many claims as possible."

Maybe this is to be expected given Social Security's massive unfunded liability. Whatever the explanation, your best posture is to assume your benefits will someday be clawed back, at least to some degree, unless you can prove they've been correctly calculated.

As noted in Chapter 1, we received an email from a disabled women desperate to have her benefits restored. She said, in part:

I was told by SSA staff in Cleburne, Texas that local office policy is to NEVER give money back AND that local office policy trumps regulations so they don't have to follow them. To this day NO ONE will discuss regulation 404.1028 with me. They refused dozens of attempts to request an in-person meeting to discuss or work through the problems. Yet, on the phone, they won't discuss the regulations either. They say they don't have access... they are on ssa.gov!

Recall, Social Security faces no penalty for making mistakes in handling your benefit claim. If it pays you too much, it will likely discover the mistake, but it may take 45 years. No matter.

If Social Security finds it has overpaid and you're 95, it will still come after you. If you're dead when it discovers the overpayment, it will go after your surviving spouse, ex-spouse, young kids, disabled kids, parents—anyone collecting a penny on your record. Indeed, it will claw back guardians who receive what the agency claims are overpayments on behalf of the children for whom they are caring, as we demonstrated in Chapter 6.

Friends Don't Threaten Friends

Apparently, each claims agent, of whom there appear to be over ten thousand, can adopt his or her own posture with respect to clawbacks. Some are, it seems, far more aggressive than others. This includes what type of threats they include in their clawback letters and how lenient they are in granting clawback waivers.

We have told many of their stories earlier in this book. By now, you should know that Social Security is not the great helpful benefactor and distributor of your well-earned benefits. But in case you jumped to the conclusion, this story encapsulates the combination of ignorance and malfeasance now entrenched in the Social Security system:

Meet Roy Farmer, a 32-year-old resident of Grand Rapids, Michigan, who Larry wrote about in *Forbes* and on his larrykotlikoff.substack.com newsletter/podcast site. The article's title says it all. "Social Security Sues 32-Year-Old for Benefits 'He' Received 21 Years Ago, at Age 11."

Roy has cerebral palsy. When he was a child, his now-deceased mom applied for Supplemental Security Income on Roy's behalf. Such benefits are available to children who are disabled and whose parents have low income.

Roy received his first clawback letter in 2021. We copy it nearby. Like almost all such letters, there is no explanation for why Social Security is demanding repayment. There is also no explanation for why Roy should be responsible for something over which he had absolutely no control and, indeed, no knowledge.

Roy, who we've met and who was featured, along with the two of us, on the *60 Minutes* exposé, is a fabulous person. He's also nobody's lunchmeat, including Social Security's. He's fighting its outrageous clawback tooth and nail. It has taken him two years to find out that the clawback stems from a Social Security determination that when he turned age 11 he was "cured of CP."

Earth to Social Security: Cerebral palsy is not curable. You can improve your ability to function via operations—Roy had three—but the disease doesn't miraculously disappear, nor does the disability. Roy

Social Security Administration
Billing Statement
Important Information

Great Lakes Program Service Center
600 West Madison Street
Chicago, Illinois 60661-2474
Date: September 8, 2021
BNC#: 21F0206K51473-01

lhnllrbhdlpllldlllhllhhlpllllphlllphlphhlllqlp
ANGELA FERRIS FOR
ROY E FARMER

Due to the coronavirus (COVID-19) pandemic, we paused the mailing
of our billing notices. We are also experiencing delays in processing
payments you may have sent us. We are working to process these
payments and to return any stale dated checks. If you owe us a payment,
please see the payment stub within this notice on ways you can repay. For
your convenience, we now offer an online payment option.

AMOUNT DUE	$4,902.00
Balance From Previous Statement	$4,902.00
New Balance	$4,902.00

PAYMENT OF NEW BALANCE OR AMOUNT DUE
MUST REACH US BY   September 23, 2021

Did You Forget?

This statement concerns an overpayment of Supplemental Security Income
payments paid to ROY E FARMER.

We have not received the payment due. Please send us the full payment right away.

**For your convenience, you can make a secure payment at www.pay.gov/
public/form/start/834689469 online. Your Remittance ID is DB58QW88XK.**

To request to repay a smaller amount monthly over a longer period of time, please
call us at the telephone number below.

If you have mailed the payment amount due within the past week, please disregard
this statement.

asked Social Security for the determination records providing the evidence that he'd functionally become disability-free at age 11. Social Security said it had lost the records.

Hence, Roy is being clawed back for a benefit his mother received, a benefit of which he had no knowledge, and a benefit over which he had no control. And now Social Security admits it has no evidence proving the clawback was legitimate. Roy continues to struggle with CP, as he has every day of his life.

When, two decades ago, Social Security sent 11-year-old Roy its clawback notice, it told him (actually his mother) that she could appeal the decision. His mother appealed the decision that he was no longer disabled. That appeal was denied, and the payments he had received during the appeal process were clawed back. But the mother never paid the amount demanded.

Now, over twenty years later, Roy is working and earning a moderate income. And Social Security is clawing back money his deceased mother did not repay at the time—$4,902.

Roy has now filed his own appeal to an administrative law judge employed by Social Security. Hence, Roy is likely to be denied yet again. At that point, Roy's recourse will be appealing to a federal district court, which can provide a hearing or summarily reject the request. He will need a lawyer for that.

Meanwhile, Roy continues to receive increasingly nasty clawback letters. The most recent such letter contained these threats.

If we don't receive the amount due, we can collect the money owed us:

- *from Federal income tax refunds*
- *from other Federal payments you may be due*
- *from your salary if you are an employee of the federal government*
- *from State income tax refunds*
- *from other State payments you may be due*

- *from future Supplemental Security Income payments*
- *from future Social Security benefits*
- *through a federal court lawsuit*
- *by ordering your employer to withhold and send us a portion of your pay.*
- *We can also report your overdue debt to credit bureaus.*

This is truly sick. And Social Security knows it's sick. When the agency was invited to appear on *60 Minutes*, it declined. Clearly, no one—not the incoming commissioner, not the acting commissioner, not any of the system's top officials—has the guts to appear on national television and discuss these issues.

CHAPTER 19

The Appeals Process — or *non*-Process!

A s Roy's case indicates, one can't simply appeal unreasonable claw-backs and expect them to be waived automatically.

The Devil Is in the Details

When you receive a clawback letter, you have 60 days to file an appeal. You can appeal for reconsideration, a waiver, or both (via submitting two requests). A reconsideration appeal is based on your contention that Social Security's clawback is mistaken; i.e., that you have always received the correct benefit payment. An example is a recent case Larry encountered. It involves a British woman who we'll call Liz, married to an American, who we'll call Richard.

Liz and Richard married several years ago. Richard was already collecting a healthy Social Security retirement benefit. After one year, Liz was eligible to collect a spousal benefit on Richard's record equal to half of his full retirement benefit. She filed and started receiving her monthly payment. Fast forward to January 2021. Liz opens their mailbox and a claw darts out grabbing her purse. Social Security is demanding she return $40,000.

Liz contacted her financial planner who contacted Social Security and ultimately Larry. Liz's clawback was, they learned, based on the Government Pension Offset provision or GPO. The GPO reduces your Social Security dependent benefit by two-thirds of your noncovered government pension. Two-thirds of Liz's pension from teaching high school *in England* exceeded her spousal benefit. This is why Social Security claimed it was paying her a benefit she should never have received.

But here's the deal. The word "government" in GPO references an American government, not a British school system. Pensions received from work abroad, including work for foreign governments or foreign companies, neither of which are examples of U.S. governments, are exempt from the GPO.

Liz filed an appeal for reconsideration because the application of the GPO in her case was clearly wrong. As we write, 18 months later, Liz has heard nothing about her appeal. The only thing she knows is that it was received by Social Security. She also knows that her monthly check has been canceled.

It's hard to know how long it will take for Liz to win her case. In the meantime, more scary clawback letters keep showing up in her mailbox and her monthly benefits have been canceled. Liz will eventually win her case. But it's already been 18 months of daily anxiety over a bill she doesn't owe and a benefit she's owed, but not receiving. And no one at Social Security is able or willing to explain what's going on.

Liz's story is a case study of the system's dysfunction and illustrates that Social Security's capacity for mistakes includes making mistakes about mistakes. And here's a well-hidden point of law that no panicked claimant would have known.

Had Liz filed for a waiver rather than reconsideration, she would have lost the waiver appeal and, it seems, lost the option to appeal for reconsideration. Appeals must be filed within 60 days. If Social Security mistakenly claws back benefits that are rightfully yours and you don't appeal the clawback for reconsideration within that time frame, you're out the money the system demands. That's beyond appalling, but, apparently, entirely true.

Inherent Dangers of Waivers

As for filing for a waiver, they are granted under two conditions. The first condition is the one we've mentioned. You need to prove that the benefits being clawed back represent overpayments due to Social Security's mistake. You also need to demonstrate, via all manner of financial documentation, from your bank account to your cable plan, that you are indigent.

Liz's hypothetical waiver appeal would have failed both parts of this test. Her overpayment wasn't a mistake made by Social Security because, well, it wasn't a mistake in the first place. Second, she's not indigent.

There is one more path to request a waiver. A waiver can be requested on the basis of "equity and good conscience." If a repayment demand goes against the intent of the Social Security Act—i.e., if it would violate equity and good conscience (equitable and conscientious behavior)—it can be waived. The application for a waiver based on equity and good conscience is more likely to be accepted if the beneficiary relied on the overpayment. Examples here include having used the overpayment to buy a home or send your child to college.

Waivers, as mentioned, are in the hands of local claims representatives. Which claims representative you end up with is the luck of the draw. If claims reps in Texas are tougher than those in Minnesota and you live in Texas, too bad for you.

But claims reps across the country routinely deny waiver requests. Social Security's unstated policy in recent decades appears to be: Deny almost all initial waiver requests and see if the beneficiary gives up. After the first waiver is denied, a second waiver appeal can be filed, again within 60 days. If that appeal is also rejected, one has 60 days to appeal to an administrative law judge (ALJ).

But these judges are judges in name only. They are under no strictures to abide by standard rules of law. Thus, the absence of due process, e.g., not providing Roy Farmer with a copy of the Social Security-appointed doctor's decision to declare him "cured" of CP, won't impact the ALJ's decision. Instead, the ALJ will surely do what ALJs routinely do in these circumstances—*deny the waiver request.*

Roy, as indicated, refuses to be a Social Security victim. If the ALJ rejects his waiver appeal, he will appeal to his local federal district court. He may also decide to sue Social Security for violating his right to due process. If so, Roy will likely used Go Fund Me or a similar platform to raise money to hire legal counsel, and we will keep you updated on our website: www.SocialSecurityHorrorStories.com. Roy's not into this for the money. Yes, the $4,902.00 constitutes a sizeable chunk of his annual take home pay. But he won't starve to death paying it. He'll be suing Social Security, if he does, on behalf of all of us.

CHAPTER 20

Keep Your Own Records

O ne of the most dismaying and disheartening results of reading all our Social Security horror stories is the abundant evidence that Social Security mismanages information it should have been collecting over the years. Of course, it finds other reasons to stonewall requests for information about its clawback decisions. But in so many ways, it admits that it cannot prove its case because it has no records. Instead, it relies on its power and impenetrable authority.

Even worse, when Social Security does deign to discuss the issues with beneficiaries, it does not keep records of those conversations. So you can never prove what was said unless you keep careful records and record your conversations.

Social Security Keeps No Record of Your Interactions

Larry joined another call recently with a Social Security representative—Ms. Arbella. She was calling John and Paula Smith (made-up names) who had been waiting for over 18 months to learn why they were being clawed back roughly $26,000. John is a 74-year-old retired teacher. He went to his local Social Security office at age 65 to file for his retirement benefit. John was fully aware that it would be reduced because he was receiving a pension from noncovered employment. He made this clear to the staffer with whom he met. The pension was coming from the Teachers Retirement System of Illinois.

The staff person told John to use the office computer to apply for his retirement benefit online. She told him to return to the window after he had submitted his form. She would review his application and double-check if everything was in order once he submitted it. John did as instructed. But Ms. Arbella claimed that John failed to indicate that he was receiving a noncovered pension.

High school social science teachers don't, in the normal course of events, lie on government forms, especially under threat of committing perjury. Ok, maybe John made a mistake. Perhaps he didn't pay close enough attention to his entries because the agent had promised to check over his application.

Larry had written up John's Social Security horror story in *Forbes*. Ms. Arbella had read it and was none too pleased. She was cold as ice. She said that John had been overpaid for nine years and she was calling to set up a payment plan. Alternatively, John and his wife could immediately pay back the entire $26,232 that they owed.

The following exchange ensued:

Larry: Do you have any record of John's meeting nine years ago?

Ms. Arbella: No. Mr. Smith can return to the office. Perhaps the staff person is still there. We don't keep track of applicants' meetings with staff.

Larry: Where is the proof that John incorrectly filled out his retirement benefit application form?

Ms. Arbella: I will send Mr. Smith a copy of his application.

Larry: You have the ability to waive this clawback based on the statute that permits waivers if the clawback would go against equity and good conscience. This clearly goes against equity and good conscience.

Megan: You can write this up in Forbes *like you did before, but I'm not going to waive this claim. The claims representative who handled Mr. Smith's waiver appeal denied it. I can't*

162

overrule that decision. We do not waive claims on the basis of equity and good conscience.

Mr. Smith can appeal the waiver denial and have a hearing with an administrative law judge. It may take up to two years for the hearing to occur. Waivers are only granted if the party requesting the waiver was not at fault. Here, Mr. Smith was at fault. He perjured himself on the form. Even if he wasn't at fault, he would need to prove he is extremely poor to be granted a waiver.

Ms. Arbella sent the Smiths a printout of the data they recorded for John. She did not send a copy of John's application. My guess is that SSA doesn't have the original application. If so, where is the direct evidence that John didn't disclose his receipt of a noncovered pension? Is this yet another violation of due process?

One might believe that an electronic summary of an electronic application would be entirely accurate,. but Social Security's computer systems are hardly foolproof. In June of 2019, Social Security mailed out patently false benefit statements to millions of workers. The statements showed that workers would receive far more in benefits if they took their retirement benefit at age 62 than if they waited till full retirement age. It seems that no one at Social Security caught this mistake until Larry wrote about it in *Forbes*. Larry has also written about people receiving bizarre estimates of widow(er)'s benefits—estimates that suggest fundamental software bugs.

Congress must force Social Security to maintain proper records of meetings with the American public. But until it does, you're on your own to prove your point in a dispute with Social Security. Here's what you should be doing regarding every interaction.

Proving Your Point

Because you're dealing with an adversary, when you meet with Social Security, either in person or on the phone, you need to record your conversations. You have the right to do so. Until Social Security modernizes its communications and tracking systems, it will be up to you to document your interactions with the agency. If you eventually want to dispute a clawback or a benefit amount that you believe is too low, it will be important to have documentation of what was said. Simple apps make this easy to do on your cell phone.

We cannot say this clearly enough: Social Security does not keep adequate records of its conversations and advice. It is perfectly legal and legitimate for you to let the person you are speaking with—either over the phone or in an office—know that you are recording this conversation so you will be able to remember it accurately.

Note: Social Security has told people it is illegal to record in a federal building. That is not true, exactly. It is illegal for a *federal employee* to record a conversation in a federal building. But you are well within your rights to tell the employee that you are recording the conversation. (See 18 U.S.C 2511(2)(d).)

If you are reaching out to Social Security by telephone, you may also have difficulty in getting the identity of a Social Security phone rep. There does not appear to be any badge number or office identification number for telephone reps, although they may give you their first name. In fact, in our experience they get offended if you want to know exactly who they are!

When you start your recording, clearly state the date and time, and your name, and ask the person to state his or her full name and department, and if possible, the city in which the office is located. Theoretically, all calls are being recorded "for clarity and training purposes" by the agency, but it likely will never be able to access them to help you with a problem.

If you have questions about anything the representative says, be sure to ask them clearly and state your concerns. Don't be afraid to do this more than once. For example, you might say: "Well, now I have mentioned that I have a teacher's pension. Are you sure that my monthly benefit includes any offsets for this pension of $XXX per month?"

Remember, you will be depending on the clarity and details of your interactions with Social Security to prove your point about any future benefits decisions or clawbacks.

Keeping Social Security Honest

Perhaps the worst nightmare of all Social Security horror stories is applying for your retirement benefit only to learn that your earnings record is incorrect. Maybe you worked three jobs and only two reported contributing FICA taxes on your behalf. Or maybe your employers properly reported, but Social Security never entered their reports of your covered earnings. Or maybe another person had your same Social Security number (Yes, this happens!) and your covered earnings were allocated to that person's work record.

If you land in this trap, the only way to escape is to have records of your earnings history going back as far as age 16. This is why we urge you to keep physical as well as electronic copies of your pay stubs for all pay periods as well as your annual W-2 forms. We also stress the importance of establishing an account at www.ssa.gov and checking your earnings record. If there is a mistake and you can prove it using pay stubs or your annual W-2s, head into Social Security and make sure it corrects your record.

We have 261 million adults in our country. Only 19 million have ssa.gov accounts. This means that only a relatively few workers are in a position to check their earnings records online. But everyone can apply for a written statement. Just go to www.ssa.gov and in the search box ask for SSA-7004. That will lead you to the form for making a written request for your earnings history.

Yes, the concern we're raising here about misinformation on earnings history impacts a very small share of beneficiaries. But you don't want to be a part of that statistic. It's essential to check your historic earnings record.

If you elect to take Social Security before your full retirement age, you face the earnings test. For the first year, there is both a monthly and annual test. If the Social Security Administration doesn't have the monthly data—from after you start collecting, it will apply the annual earnings test, which could reduce your current benefit. Thus, in the first year of early retirement, you should report your monthly earnings to SSA on a timely basis.

CHAPTER 21

Social Security Is Dysfunctional

t's not easy to make almost a quarter of a million benefit payment mistakes year in and year out. How can Social Security be this inept? The answer lies in another dirty little secret that Social Security has spent decades hiding. For millions of us, Social Security simply doesn't have the information it needs to correctly calculate our benefits. In these cases, it effectively relies on us to tell it what to pay us. But since it can't check that the information we are providing is accurate, it doesn't want us to know that it doesn't know it doesn't know.

Social Security's staff is underpaid, overworked, and undertrained. We know from experience that half of their answers to questions, no matter how simple, are either dead wrong, half wrong, or misleading. Yes, the bubbly young staffer, who you just met at the local office or on the phone, couldn't have been nicer. But she may have just spent the last hour with you:

- Conning you out of hundreds of thousands of dollars via the widows scam.
- Failing to check that your retirement benefit was properly subjected to the WEP.
- Failing to ask about available divorced spousal benefits when you filed for retirement benefits.
- Detailing the earnings test but uttering not a peep about the adjustment of the reduction factor.
- Suggesting, incorrectly, that you can't suspend your retirement benefit at full retirement age.

- Denying you divorced widow(er)'s benefits even though you remarried after age 60.
- Limiting your benefits by applying the wrong family benefit maximum.
- Saying nothing about the monthly earnings test available when first filing for retirement benefits.
- Pushing you to take benefits early to ensure you won't lose them.
- Making dozens of other major and minor mistakes of commission and omission.

Social Security Doesn't Want Us to Know It Doesn't Know

At any given point in time, 7 percent, or roughly 5 million, U.S. workers are employed in the non-Social Security-covered sector. Once in retirement, their benefits will be subject to the WEP and GPO, as described in Chapter 4. A key point discussed in *Get What's Yours* is that neither the WEP nor GPO is applied until workers start receiving their noncovered pension or initiate their first withdrawal. This means they can receive benefits free of the WEP or GPO by deferring, if possible, taking their noncovered pension or waiting to start their noncovered retirement account withdrawals.

That's potentially a very big deal—one that can be examined using Larry's MaxiFi Planner or MMSS software. But the relevant point here is that Social Security needs to know two things: *when* the noncovered pension or noncovered pension equivalent (403b, for example) is paid out and the *amount* paid. To ensure it doesn't overpay, Social Security needs to know the noncovered pension being paid starting each month the pension is received. As for noncovered pension equivalents, Social Security needs to know the amount of the account balance when the noncovered retirement account was first tapped as well as the date of the first withdrawal, even if it's only a penny.

Now here's the key point. If you're receiving a pension from an employer, you annually receive a 1099 form for your taxes. Noncovered employers also send a copy of this 1099 to the IRS. And if you make a retirement plan withdrawal, your plan custodian sends a copy of the 1099 to you and to the IRS.

But, importantly, Social Security does *not* receive a copy of these distributions from noncovered employers and plans. Nor are they forwarded to Social Security from the IRS.

Moreover, Social Security does not reach out to ask noncovered employers to disclose their noncovered pension payouts, nor the first date of withdrawal from a noncovered retirement account along with the account balance at that point in time.

Thus, Social Security is completely in the dark when it comes to correctly calculating the WEP and GPO!

Stated differently, unless you tell Social Security the amount of your noncovered pension in the first month it arrives and/or the balance amount of your noncovered retirement account (such as a 403(b) in the first month you initiate a withdrawal from such accounts, it can't apply the WEP or GPO. This means Social Security will overpay you. And, if Social Security later learns this information, it will automatically initiate a clawback.

Social Security is hardly going out of its way to demand this information from you. There is no line in its script that says: *Tell us about your noncovered benefits so we won't overpay you. We don't have any way of not overpaying you if you don't tell us.*

In fact, you could easily overlook this provision. Here's what Social Security's new, online benefits explanation says about noncovered earnings.

Earnings Not Covered by Social Security

You may also have earnings from work not covered by Social Security, where you did not pay Social Security taxes. This work may have been for federal, state, or local government or in a foreign country. If you participate in a retirement plan or receive a pension based on work for which you did not pay Social Security tax, it could lower your benefits. Learn more at ssa.gov/gpo-wep.

The link says nothing about contacting Social Security when you start receiving a noncovered pension or distribution from a noncovered retirement account. Yes, benefit application forms ask about past noncovered employment. But they do so in a manner almost guaranteed to produce an overpayment. Take the retirement benefit application. It first asks:

> "Are you entitled to, or do you expect to be entitled to, a pension or annuity (or a lump sum in place of a pension or annuity) based on your work after 1956 not covered by Social Security?"

If you say yes, the form asks when you expect to become entitled. Next then the forms states:

> "I agree to promptly notify the Social Security Administration if I become entitled to a pension, an annuity, or a lump-sum payment based on my employment not covered by Social Security or if such pension or annuity stops."

If you are going to receive noncovered retirement income in the future, you'll surely believe that your answer to the prior question fulfills your reporting requirement. But the word "entitled" is Social Security's inside baseball language. It refers to actually collecting. It doesn't refer to eligibility to collect, which is the everyday reading of the word entitled. In short, it would be easy for an applicant who will collect a noncovered pension next year to indicate this and when next year is here not to think they have any special reporting obligation.

The Information Catch 22

Both of us think there should be a statute of limitation on clawbacks. If Social Security can't fix its mistakes in, say, 18 months, it should leave its clawback targets in financial peace. But were it to adopt this policy, it would need to do what it should have been doing forever—independently collecting the information it needs to apply the WEP and GPO correctly and on time. Without that information, a statute of limitations would provide beneficiaries impacted by the WEP or the GPO an incentive to not inform Social Security when the noncovered funds arrive.

In short, given its information limitations, (and similar limitations apply to a far wider range of benefit payments than noncovered pensions/equivalents), the agency may view itself as trapped into clawing back with no time limit, indeed beyond the grave. Of course, with the ability to claw back with no time limit, the agency has little incentive to gather the information it needs directly from noncovered employers. Hence, a statute of limitations is surely the right solution to compel Social Security to do its job properly.

Protecting Yourself Against Social Security's Ignorance

If Social Security is this incompetent—relying on millions of Americans to tell it things it should determine on its own, our only answer is to send the agency what it needs to know. Yes, you can tell Social Security you are going to collect, say, a noncovered pension at date X of size Y. It won't matter. Social Security needs to know for sure when date X occurs and the precise size of Y.

To be absolutely safe, you need to transmit the information Social Security needs on a monthly basis. For example, if you receive a noncovered pension each month of $1,000, you need, each month, to send a copy of the receipt for the $1,000 to Social Security via certified mail, return receipt requested. You also need to keep a diary of such transmissions. Even better, you can go to your local Social Security office each month and ask them to stamp two copies of your transmission— one they keep, one you keep.

You also want to report every penny of retirement income received from noncovered employers. Again, send in copies of the payment statements, check stubs, etc., to Social Security by certified mail, return signature required. Bear in mind that Social Security doesn't have this information and that when it learns through whatever means it uses, you'll be clawed back unless you tell it exactly what you are receiving at the time you are receiving it.

If this sounds absolutely nuts, it is. But we can't think of any other way Social Security will receive what it needs to make the correct benefit calculations. We'll discuss this more below, but for now we want to raise two further key points.

First, even if you send Social Security precisely the information it demands at precisely the right time, there is no guarantee the information won't be lost, misused, or applied months or years beyond when it should.

Second, unless you drive yourself nuts transmitting the information that Social Security and/or Congress is too inept to collect on its own, you may end up being underpaid. Here's an example:

Suppose you are a retired Massachusetts school teacher receiving a noncovered monthly pension of $3,000. Assume this pension is not inflation adjusted. Also assume you're a widow whose widow's benefit equals $1,800. The GPO will zap your widow's benefit by two-thirds of your noncovered pension. Two-thirds of $3,000 is $2,000. Since $2,000 exceeds $1,800, your widow's benefit is wiped out by the GPO. But, over time, the $1,800 will grow due to annual COLAs (cost of living adjustments). *As soon as the $1,800 exceeds $2,000, your GPO'd widow's benefit will become positive!*

Who knows if Social Security will recompute your widow's benefit every month based on the static monthly $3,000 pension. But one thing is clear. If you don't convey, over time, by certified mail, registered receipt requested, that your noncovered monthly pension is still $3,000, you'll have little hope of getting Social Security to pay you what it owes.

Don't Trust—Don't Ask!

There is only one way to ensure you receive fully correct answers to your Social Security questions from Social Security's staff. Don't ask them a single question, not even the time of day. Asking Social Security anything is asking for trouble. Your future benefits are surely your first, second, or third largest retirement asset. Their maximization is far too important to your financial well-being, if not your survival, to let the "experts" do what they do worst—cost you a ton of money.

You spend a fortune over your lifetime on your morning coffee, on your online subscriptions, and perhaps on dining out. Can we ask you to invest just a fraction of that money and time into preserving the Social Security benefits you have earned and deserve? Here's how to proceed:

Got $2.95? That's what it takes to buy a used copy of *Get What's Yours: The Secrets to Maxing Out Your Social Security (GWY)*. *GWY* is Larry's 2016 co-authored book about Social Security's rules upon rules upon rules. Thanks to Larry's co-authors, *PBS NewsHour*'s economics correspondent, Paul Solman and long-time personal finance journalist Phillip Moeller, the book is a surprisingly fun read. You can easily find it on Amazon.

And if you don't want to read it, just run the software at www. MaximizeMySocialSecurity.com, (cost: $39), which you'll want to do in any case. *GWY*, together with this book, will arm you to do battle with Social Security, which, unfortunately, is highly likely.

MaximizeMySocialSecurity is an online calculator that has been run by tens of thousands of households. If you go to the website, you'll see one glowing testimonial after another. To use MMSS effectively, you'll need to input or import your earnings record. And you'll want to be fully accurate about your noncovered pensions and noncovered retirement accounts. The program is extremely user-friendly. It handles the entire gamut of benefits (apart from parent benefits) and incorporates all Social Security provisions, including the earnings test and Adjustment of the Reduction Factor, the WEP, and the GPO. MMSS is meticulous in handling Social Security's myriad benefit rules. The only exception is that it doesn't calculate disability benefits.

The cost of MMSS is trivial relative to the amount of money any Social Security beneficiary has at stake. Larry's company's main software tool is called *MaxiFi Planner* (at www.Maxifi.com). Since Larry is an economist, *MaxiFi Planner* does economics-based financial planning. This includes getting Social Security right. MMSS uses MaxiFi's Social Security code to guide households who just need help figuring out what benefits are theirs to collect and how best to collect them.

Specifically, like MaxiFi, MMSS determines what benefits a household should collect and when to maximize one's lifetime benefits.

Larry started his company, Economic Security Planning, in 1993. It was the first company to provide a fully detailed Social Security lifetime benefit calculator. Yes, there are many free benefit calculators available. AARP has one, for example. They aren't reliable. Why? Because they aren't asking sufficiently detailed questions to produce correct results. Indeed, as explained earlier, Social Security's own benefit calculators aren't to be trusted.

Action Is the Only Reaction

S ocial Security does enormous good. But unbeknownst to most of us, Social Security has a scary side. It employs over 60,000 bureaucrats, precious few of whom are even remotely equipped to deal with the system's mind-numbing complexity. Moreover, the system lacks critical data needed to calculate benefits correctly for millions of beneficiaries.

The combination of byzantine rules, hopeless staff, and missing data spell all manner of benefit mistakes—many that take years or decades to discover. When that happens to you, good luck getting a cogent explanation, let alone evidentiary proof that the mistake is not, itself, in error. And a quick, reasonable fix by Social Security of its own mistake? That's waiting for hell to freeze over. No private company would last a week treating its customers in this horrific fashion.

Social Security has an answer. Actions speak louder than words. Here's what Social Security's actions say:

We make overpayment errors, and you pay for them. Massive or minor. It makes no difference. When we find a mistake or what we think is a mistake, we will mail you a letter—a clawback letter, which, all too often, contains horrific news: You owe us lots of money!

Don't blame us. You should have learned our hundreds of thousands of rules and told us what to pay you. You should have realized, without our telling you, that we're unequipped, data wise, to get many things right. Plus, you should have gotten a PhD in filling out our forms so we couldn't entrap you as easily as we did.

And, yes, many of you, whether mentally or physically impaired, should have made it to the post office every month and sent us certified mail about your earnings, non-covered pensions, changed marital status, child's graduation date, and plenty of other essential things we can't bother, after 88 years, to collect on our own. And yes, we may permanently ignore what you sent us or opened your communications years later, but, hey, we're busy.

As for "scams," we don't run scams. We're straight by our book. Yes, it's a massive book, and written in a foreign language where the word "entitled" has a wholly different meaning than the word "eligible." We didn't write the law, we just interpreted it to our financial advantage, made up instructions for our staff, and told them to follow orders. They can be good soldiers—or they can go work elsewhere.

Sexist? There's not a single word in our multitudinous rules that is sexist. You'll see no utterance of the words male or female. A woman staying home to raise three kids whose husband divorces her a day before her 10th anniversary— depriving her of every penny of future spousal and widows benefits? Well, she could have been nicer and kept her hubby happy. If she split up her family, well, shame on her. Our laws were written by men in the 1950s. They knew how to treat faithful women well and punish the rest, including those who remarried before age 60.

We at Social Security could go on, but here's the bottom line. Every awful thing we do to you is your fault. That's our working principle. It's worked for 88 years and will work for another 88 years. So, you just apologize, pay up, and stop appealing our decisions. The appeals process is designed for punishment, not justice.

This captures the system's arrogance and monopoly on power. No one, not even individual members of Congress, can help individual constituents. Of course, collectively, Congress can change things overnight. With your help, they will!

From the recipient's perspective, these clawback letters read as follows:

Hello. This is Social Security. We overpaid you $$$ for reasons we can't bother to disclose, let alone explain, let alone prove. Even if this mistake was our mistake, you owe us the money. Yes, you can request we waive our clawback. You can even appeal our judgment. But we are masters of the runaround and specialists in denial.

So, don't hold your breath waiting for our response or to prove a thing. We'll get around to it in a year or two. In the meantime, please hand over the $$$ or we will immediately cut any benefit you are receiving or grab your tax refund or garnish your wages. Or, if we so choose, we'll give you our special treatment: We'll sue you.

The Rest of the Story—
The Agency Has the Power to End Clawbacks

Eliminating Social Security's scams requires Congressional action. As for clawbacks, Social Security can stop them immediately. How so? The law gives Social Security wide discretion on how to handle clawbacks. This assessment is based on our discussions with lawyers, Social Security officials, Social Security staff, and former technical assistants. The precise implementation of clawbacks is at the agency's discretion. It's not codified in law.

But the real revelation comes from Social Security's action when confronted with the most embarrassing of these horror stories. When the level of Agency embarrassment gets sufficiently high—eg., a headline proclaiming Social Security suing a six-year-old orphan—someone at the top makes a call and things get fixed.

Social Security has fixers in place assigned to handle its worst cases of abuse, *provided they become public*. A truly horrific story that makes the press leads to action within days, sometimes hours.

The reason Social Security can fix its worst abuses is the same reason it can fix *all* its abuses, if it chooses. *It has the legal authority to do so.* The actual law—statute and official regulations—are clear to anyone who wants to read their words with an open mind and a caring heart. Social Security is legally required to uphold the intent of its enabling legislation. It is enjoined to act in accord with "equity" and in accord with "good conscience."

Change Can Happen

The first version of *Get What's Yours* was published in February 2015. Within three weeks it was #1 on Amazon's best seller list. It stayed there for nine days and remained on Amazon's top-10 list for the following seven months—through November 2015. That's when Congress decided too many people were following the book's advice and amended the law.

Senior Social Security officials told Larry that Congress decided that *GWY* was costing the system too much money because it revealed perfectly legal claiming strategies. They couldn't ban the book. Instead, they eliminated an important benefit-increasing strategy called *file and suspend*, whose use the book was, in part, explaining.

They did this effectively in the dead of a Sunday night, releasing the amendments that would be put up for a vote the following Friday. Larry realized that the amendments would lead to a cut in benefits for many beneficiaries come April. He wrote a column for *Forbes* on Monday morning. By Monday afternoon, Congress had created amendments to the amendments, which grandfathered people born before January 1, 1954.

In any case, Larry and his co-authors were forced to rewrite their book. The revised version of *GWY* was published in 2016. Since there have been literally no changes in Social Security rules since those made in 2015, the book remains fully up to date. But this is clear proof that enough public pressure can cause change!

Calling the Commissioner to Action

Here are the policies we would implement on Day 1 were we in charge of Social Security.

- **Statute of Limitations.** If Social Security makes a mistake that it fails to detect within 18 months, the liability should fall on the agency. This time limit should include errors arising from data Social Security can collect on its own, rather than depend on participants, many older, disabled, and underaged, to provide information that complies with often-indecipherable instructions.

- **Client Meetings.** Social Security should record all client meetings, whether in person or by telephone. Transcripts of these records should be produced digitally, stored in each client's electronic file, and accessible to each client on a secure gateway. Each meeting should record the Social Security staffer's identification number.

- **Ending Runarounds.** Every Social Security staffer assigned to interact with clients must be able to provide all clients full customer support in real time. With instantly accessible records, claimants should no longer have to visit several different offices, or hope for a return phone call, to get a response to their questions or problems.

- **Social Security Data Retrieval.** Social Security must collect all information needed to correctly calculate their client's basic benefits, particularly WEP and GPO data, directly from noncovered employers. No benefit calculations should depend on data provided by clients. Income reported from public pensions should be transmitted automatically to Social Security, where it may reduce benefits as a result of pension offsets.

- **Ombudsman.** The IRS has successful created a Taxpayer Assistance Center. Social Security could easily copy this model. Social Security's Office of the Ombudsman would be authorized to resolve mistakes without forcing clients to resort to the appeals process, saving both money and heartache.

- **Timing of Appeals.** Social Security should pay a fine to clients who fail to receive a hearing on their appeals within a year. Currently, the process may take two years, or longer.

- **Clawback Documentation.** All clawback notices should fully explain their reason and provide supporting proof that would be required in a court of law under rules of due process.

- **Administrative Law Judges.** The administrative law judges that hear appeals must be truly independent. They should be members of the federal judiciary, not Social Security's hired hands. Their performance should be judged based on how quickly they adjudicate cases and how humanely they treat the public, not on how much money they claw back for the system.

Insistence on Decency

"At long last, have you no sense of decency?" were the words uttered by U.S. Army Counsel Jack Welch at the infamous McCarthy hearings—nine words that struck a deep chord with the American public and ended McCarthy's witch hunt.

We have similar words for those ultimately responsible for Social Security's disgraces.

At long last, members of Congress, have you no sense of shame—letting Social Security sue six-year olds, claw back overpayments made 45 years ago, kick elderly widows to the street, treat retired school teachers as criminals, and send massive bills to disabled workers for earning a few extra bucks—an innocent mistake detected a decade after the "transgression"?

And have you no shame in running the mother of all Ponzi schemes—one that is dumping $65.9 trillion worth of red ink in our children's laps. And what about all the other scams, many highly misogynistic, that are deterring millions of early beneficiaries from returning to work, that are often conning widows out of vital income, that are deceiving low-wage *spouses into believing their FICA contributions will deliver extra benefits, that are inducing workers to take benefits far too early, and more?*

Reasons We Wrote the Book

This book is meant to alarm and alert the public—to protect itself from, of all things, Social Security. It's meant to expose Social Security's Commissioner to intense public scrutiny. It's designed to activate the media to do the job it's generally failed to do: Report the system's abuses—big and small and not for a single news cycle. To its enormous credit, *60 Minutes* has taken the lead in their 2023 exposé of Social Security's clawbacks. Other media need to cover and stay on this story.

This book's other primary objective is meant to blow the co-conspirators' cover, starting with Congress. Its members can no longer plead ignorance of Social Security's systemic malfeasance. It's meant to blow the agency's cover—its cop-out that it's just following the law. It's meant to blow the President's cover—that the only problems with Social Security are financial. And it's meant to get Social Security's trustees to, at long last, do their jobs, not just meet in a fancy room, over a fancy lunch, to sign an annual report whose most important figure—the system's $65.9 trillion unfunded liability—they have buried deep in the Appendix far from the public's eye.

Our Collective Social Security Protection Plan

Social Security is broke. It's broke financially, it's broke technologically, and it's broke morally. Any institution that admits, however secretively, to having $65.9 trillion in red ink and to making over 200,000 mistakes annually is, frankly, a disgrace. And any social-protection agency that causes the human suffering described here has lost its soul and abandoned its mission.

Unfortunately, the only way to fix Social Security is via public pressure—on the agency, on its trustees, on Congress, and on the President. Galvanizing public outrage is why we wrote this book. And it's why we are appealing to you to do these simple things.

- **First**, warn everyone in your social network that Social Security can be extremely dangerous to their financial health. If you're informing your network of friends, relatives, and colleagues, please include a link to the book's listing on Amazon. (We chose to self-publish to get the book out faster and at a far lower price than a publisher would charge.)

- **Second**, ask your network to watch the *60 Minutes* segment (https://www.cbsnews.com/60-minutes/) and spread that link via Facebook, X (Twitter), LinkedIn, TikTok, and all their other social media outlets. As a group, we can reach everyone in the country literally in a few seconds! We are, in a word, POWERFUL.

- **Third**, ask your network to read this book and then mail their copy—or a link—to one of their members of Congress. If they can swing it, ask them to mail copies to both of their Senators and their Congressperson.

- **Fourth**, ask them to dig even deeper and send the book to the President, and to the six trustees of Social Security, including the Secretary of the Treasury, who is Social Security's Chief Trustee.

Take these four simple steps and everyone in the country will learn overnight that Social Security has turned financial malfeasance into an art form. As for members of Congress, their offices will be over-whelmed with a book entitled *Social Security Horror Stories*. The message to Congress will be loud and clear: *If you continue to kick the Social Security can down the road, we, the people, will kick your can out of office!*

Let's Use Our Power Together!

We have our list of solutions. It's not just clawbacks. It's the scams, as well. It's saving the system for our children and grandchildren. But, in truth nothing will get fixed unless we go after the soft underbelly of the Agency and its political enablers—*EMBARRASSMENT.*

Our collective task is simple: Embarrass Social Security's Commissioner, embarrass the politicians, embarrass the President, and embarrass the Trustees. And keep embarrassing them until they realize that leaving Social Security's myriad problems "off the table" is a ticket out of Washington. With enough bad press about these horror stories, behavior will change quickly.

If you are a victim, please enter your personal horror story at www.SocialSecurityHorrorStories.com. We'll only post your first name, but please register with your email (which will remain private) so we can update you on developments. At this website, we will post links to news, legislation, and policy changes.

As the number of horror stories grows and grows, media attention will grow as well. That spells continual embarrassment, which is our secret weapon. For our part, we will continue advocating on your behalf with Social Security, Congress, and the media. Working together we can, at long last, force Social Security to live up to its name.

www.ingramcontent.com/pod-product-compliance
Lightning Source LLC
Chambersburg PA
CBHW060555200326
41521CB00007B/578